The best of
TALLINN

KELVIE

NEW
HOLLAND

9/2164757

GLOBETROTTER™

First edition published in 2009
by New Holland Publishers (UK) Ltd
London • Cape Town • Sydney • Auckland
10 9 8 7 6 5 4 3 2 1

website: www.newhollandpublishers.com

Garfield House, 86 Edgware Road
London W2 2EA, United Kingdom

80 McKenzie Street
Cape Town 8001, South Africa

Unit 1, 66 Gibbes Street
Chatswood, NSW 2067, Australia

218 Lake Road, Northcote
Auckland, New Zealand

Distributed in the USA by
The Globe Pequot Press, Connecticut

Publishing Manager: Thea Grobbelaar
DTP Cartographic Manager: Genené Hart
Editor: Thea Grobbelaar
Designer: Nicole Bannister
Cartographer: Nicole Bannister
Picture Researcher: Shavonne Govender
Proofreader: Carla Zietsman
Reproduction by Resolution (Cape Town)
Printed and bound by Times Offset (M) Sdn. Bhd.,
Malaysia.

This guidebook has been written by independent authors and updaters. The information
therein represents their impartial opinion, and
neither they nor the publishers accept payment
in return for including in the book or writing
more favourable reviews of any of the establish-
ments. Whilst every effort has been made to
ensure that this guidebook is as accurate and up
to date as possible, please be aware that the
facts quoted are subject to change, particularly
the price of food, transport and accommodation. The Publisher accepts no responsibility or
liability for any loss, injury or inconvenience
incurred by readers or travellers using this guide.

Photographic Credits:
Russell Young/jonarnold: title page;
Robin McKelvie: pages 6, 10, 13, 14, 19, 22,
26, 30, 36, 38, 41, 47, 50, 53, 62, 69, 75, 78,
80, 81, 82, 84; **Pictures Colour Library:**
pages 7, 11, 12, 20, 23, 25, 27, 32, 54, 64;
Darby Sawchuk: pages 15, 16, 21, 24, 39;
Jon Smith: cover, pages 17, 18, 28, 34, 44,
49, 66, 72, 77.

Front Cover: *Viru Gates mark the eastern
entrance into Tallinn's Old Town.*
Title Page: *Colourful traditional costumes are
worn at Estonian festivals.*

CONTENTS

MAKE THE MOST OF YOUR GUIDE

Reading these two pages will help you to get the most out of your guide and save you time when using it. Sites discussed in the text are cross-referenced with the cover maps – for example, the reference 'Map B–C3' refers to the Greater Tallinn Map (Map B), column C, row 3. Use the Map Plan below to quickly locate the map you need.

MAP PLAN

Outside Back Cover   Outside Front Cover

Inside Front Cover   Inside Back Cover

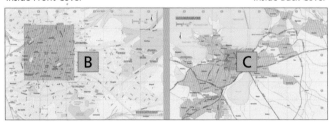

THE BIGGER PICTURE

Key to Map Plan

A – Tallinn Old Town
B – Greater Tallinn
C – Around Tallinn
D – Excursions
E – Tallinn Public Transport

Key to Symbols

✉ – address

☎ – telephone

📠 – fax

🖥 – website

📧 – e-mail address

🕐 – opening times

💰 – entry fee

🍴 – restaurants nearby

🚌 – transport

Map Legend

motorway		main road	
national road		road	
main road		city wall	
railway		built-up area	
route number	39 5	building of interest	
international boundary		post office	✉
country name	*ESTONIA*	viewpoint	𝓴
provincial boundary		hotel	Ⓗ SCHLOSSLE
province name	*Harjumaa*	parking	🅿
river and dam	*Ainu*	police station	•
ferry	– – –	hospital	⊕
city	☐ TALLINN	bus terminus	🚍
major town	⊙ Tartu	library	📖
town	○ Maardu	one-way street	→
large village	◎ Rapla	place of worship	△ Niguliste kirik
village	○ Sääre	tourist information	🅸
place of interest	★ *Palmse Mõis*	museum	■
airport	✈ ✈	shopping centre	Ⓢ *Tallinna Kaubamaja*
park & garden	■	gate	●–●
		embassy	🚩
		market	■

Keep us Current

Travel information is apt to change, which is why we regularly update our guides. We'd be most grateful to receive feedback from you if you've noted something we should include in our updates. If you have any new information, please share it with us by writing to the Publishing Manager, Globetrotter, at the office nearest to you (addresses on the imprint page of this guide). The most significant contribution to each new edition will be rewarded with a free copy of the updated guide.

Above: *The distinctive Estonian flag flying from Toompea Hill.*

TALLINN

Tallinn boasts one of Europe's most stunning old towns. The vaulting church spires, the unmistakable onion domes of its Orthodox Cathedral, the ancient fortifications and a collage of Baroque and medieval buildings unite to form a postcard-perfect picture.

One of the best ways to get a feel for Tallinn is by simply meandering around its cobbled Old Town streets, sifting through the layers of history and taking time to appreciate the stunning architecture that greets every step. Those who want to get in and about the city are also catered for by myriad museums, cultural venues and a wealth of bustling cafés, bars and nightclubs.

Perhaps unsurprisingly the Estonian capital has long been earning positive comparisons to Prague. Though to simply compare this historic gem to the Czech capital does not do the city justice. Nestled in the northeastern extremity of Europe, Tallinn enjoys an attractive and strategic location on the shores of the Baltic Sea. Less 'discovered' than its Czech counterpart, the Estonian capital is also still a city that is very much lived in and enjoyed by the locals.

Since breaking free from the shackles of Soviet rule in 1991 Tallinn has more than made up for five decades of communist-era deprivations, effortlessly adapting to capitalism and embracing new technologies, which means you never have to look too hard to find an Internet terminal or Wi-Fi hotspot in 'E-stonia'.

A Nordic Capital?

Many Estonians, especially in Tallinn, have always felt that they are a Nordic rather than a Baltic people, with closer ties to Scandinavia than to the Baltic nations to the south. This is not just cultural elitism, but a genuine feeling that the Scandinavian mindset and way of doing things is much closer than, say, the Latvian. There have been moves in recent years to make the Estonian flag a Scandinavian-style cross, as well as growing cultural and economic links with the north, though whether Estonia will form any stronger political links with Scandinavia remains to be seen.

THE LAND

The Land

Tallinn is the smallest of the three Baltic capitals (Tallinn, Rīga and Vilnius). **Vanalinn** (Tallinn's Old Town) is the city's main tourist drawcard and is divided into two parts. The **Lower Town** climbs the gentle slope towards Toompea, while **Toompea Hill** itself has a much steeper gradient and is home to iconic sights like its eponymous castle and the Alexander Nevsky Cathedral. This stunning Old Town secured Tallinn a well-deserved place on UNESCO's World Heritage List back in 1997.

The Estonian capital's modern **business heart** is located just southeast of Vanalinn. Here the landscape is dramatically different, with an ever-increasing number of modern skyscrapers stretching for the heavens and slick business hotels vying for corporate clients.

Following the coastal road east from the Old Town takes visitors to some of Tallinn's further-flung attractions, including a handful of museums and the opulent Kadriorg Palace. For those who want to relax and unwind, Tallinn also boasts around 40km^2 (15 sq miles) of parkland and a handful of modern-day spas.

Climate

Tallinn has a temperate climate. In summer the average temperature is around 15°C (59°F), with the mercury reaching 20–25°C (68–77°F) during the day. In the main tourist season days are also long and sunny, with June, July and August averaging approximately eight hours of sunshine and midsummer's day affording around 18 hours of daylight. During this time the

---

Breaking Away
Despite the fact that many Estonians have lived much of their life under Soviet rule and can speak Russian, few these days are keen to admit it, let alone talk about it. A certain amount of understandable revisionism has swept through the country, with images of Russian leaders dislodged and the Russian language being vanquished from signs and abandoned in schools. In recent years there have been grumblings from some older people that some aspects of life were better in Soviet times, but few genuinely hanker after a return to the communist days.

Below: *The park at Toompea Castle is a great place to relax in summer.*

city's colourful bars and cafés spill out onto the Old Town streets. In contrast, winter days are short and cold with average temperatures of just -3°C (27°F).

History in Brief

Although it has been inhabited since the 9th century and was first marked on a map in the middle of the 12th century, accurate records of Tallinn's historical development only date back to 1219 when Denmark seized control of the north of Estonia, including its present-day capital. The invaders erected a defensive fortification on Toompea Hill and Tallinn's Old Town gradually spread out from here. This early castle served not only to protect the city, but also gave it its name – apparently Tallinn is a derivative of *Taani Linnus*, which translates as 'Danish Castle'.

Just eight years later the city temporarily fell under the control of German knights who held sway in Tallinn until 1238. During this period the Estonian capital saw an influx of German settlers who, as a majority until the mid-19th century, held considerable sway over the city for centuries after. The influence of German merchants also saw Tallinn thrive as an important trading hub and the city was admitted to the Hanseatic League (a pan-Baltic German trading alliance) in 1248. During the 14th century the Danish King actually sold his northern Estonian territory to the Teutonic Knights.

As time passed the Poles, Swedes, Russians and Danes all fought for control over Estonia, and the country was conquered by Sweden in 1561. Swedish dominion eventually ended 149 years later when the Swedes gave Tallinn to the Russians in 1710.

Simmering beneath the surface of these momentous shifts in power was a gradual awakening of an Estonian national conscious-ness, with Tallinn at the forefront. Key events included the publication of the first Estonian-language book in 1525 and the 1793 transla-tion of the Bible into Estonian.

At the end of World War I Estonia declared itself (in Tallinn) independent. This resulted in the occupation of the city by German troops and a two-year war, commonly referred to as the **War of Independence**, with Russia. It may have come at a price, but power was finally ceded to Tallinn in 1920. World War II, how-ever, signalled the end of Estonian autonomy, with the country passing between Nazi Germany and Soviet Russia before being absorbed within the USSR in 1944.

The next 50 years were harsh ones for Estonians everywhere, with mass deporta-tions to Siberia and the flight of thousands of refugees both characteristic of the earlier years of occupation. Although the political scene settled down, many of the capital's inhabitants were far from happy with the **communist Soviet regime**, though it was not until 1987 that the first overt anti-Russian demonstrations were staged. Protests con-tinued over the next three years, in a period dubbed the **Singing Revolution** (*see* panel).

Finally in March 1991 the majority of Estonians voted for independence once again. The failed coup at the Kremlin in the summer of that year greatly helped their cause and Tallinn became the capital of the autonomous **Republic of Estonia**, as recog-nized by Russia, on 6 September 1991. In 2004 Tallinn led Estonia into both NATO and the European Union.

> **Singing Revolution**
> The struggle to free Estonia, Latvia and Lithuania from Soviet rule in the late 1980s and early 1990s has now become rather romantically known as the 'Singing Revolu-tion'. The term was coined by Estonian artist **Heinz Valk** to describe the flowering movement of mass song festivals and singing demonstrations that swept through the region between 1987 and 1991 in a re-awakening of national-ism that became an integral part of the road towards inde-pendence, with Estonia at the forefront. In an impressive act of defi-ance around 500,000 Estonians (approxi-mately a third of the country's population) attended the 1990 Song Festival (the first conducted in Estonian since World War II).

Above: *The Estonian Parliament is known as the Riigikogu.*
Opposite: *A lovely Estonian girl in traditional dress.*

Government and Economy

Estonia is a parliamentary democracy with separate executive and legislative bodies. The former, which co-ordinates the daily running of the country, is led by the prime minister. The **Riigikogu** (Estonian parliament) has 101 members and, although it has been sitting under various regimes for almost 90 years, the first elections of the Democratic Republic of Estonia were not held until 1992.

Elections take place every four years and any Estonian citizen over the age of 18 is allowed to vote. Members of parliament are elected from 12 administrative regions. Estonia also has a president.

By no means a poor 'Eastern European country', Estonia enjoys a higher Gross National Income (GNI) per capita than Latvia and Lithuania, as well as fellow EU members Poland, Slovakia and Hungary. The country's post-independence **economic growth** has averaged around 6% per annum, with the government forecasting growth of 7–8% each year in the short-term future.

A stable economy and Estonia's favourable tax system have also stimulated international trade relationships and encouraged significant levels of investment.

The People

Many ethnic Estonians have a strong sense of national identity, seeing themselves as a sort of bridge between Scandinavia and the

Estonian Flag
The Estonian tricolour is a striking flag made up of equal horizontal segments of blue, black and white from top to bottom respectively. Interestingly, it first emerged as a student flag in Tartu in the 1880s before first being hoisted as the flag of the independent nation in 1918. It fluttered above Tallinn and around the country until the Russians swept through in 1940 and it did not return until independence.

Baltics. This is more than a simple geographical fact, but also comes across in their efficient attitude to business and a 'can do' approach.

Language
Estonian is a branch of the Finno-Ugric family of languages. It is a very tricky language to learn, with 14 noun cases, but locals will appreciate your efforts, even if you can only master simple pleasantries. A lot of modern English words are creeping into Estonian and many people in Tallinn, particularly the younger generations, speak fluent English. For those who intend to travel elsewhere in Estonia, the further away from the capital you get the lower the proportion of English speakers. Finnish and Russian are also widely spoken.

Religion
Religious affiliations within Estonia broadly mirror the country's ethnic make up (around 70% of the population is Estonian and 25% Russian. The picture in the capital (population approaching 400,000) is slightly different with just over half of the city's residents being ethnic Estonian and around a quarter Russian. This means that in Tallinn (and countrywide) the **Lutheran** faith has the biggest number of adherents, followed by the **Russian Orthodox Church**. The city is also home to sizeable Ukrainian, Belarussian and Finnish **minorities** who have their own religious preferences.

The Arts
Estonia has a strong folk culture that runs parallel to and complements its interest in high culture,

Estonian Pronunciation
Accented letters, double vowels and additional vowels deter many people from attempting to speak Estonian. Every letter is clearly pronounced and there is a subtle stress on the first syllable. Getting your head (and tongue) around the different sound lengths is the hardest aspect of Estonian pronunciation. For a long vowel sound the corresponding letter is doubled, so a long 'a' sound is written '**aa**', etc. The vowel **õ** is very difficult to pronounce if you are not Estonian; try something that approximates the '**o**' sound in '**o**wn'. Other accented letters are pronounced like the sound given in bold, e.g. **ä** as in l**ai**r, **ö** as in y**ea**rn, **š** as in **sh**ort, and **ž** as in trea**s**ure.

with classical performances gracing the stages of more than a dozen theatres and concert halls in Tallinn, as well as the country's second city, Tartu. During the 19th century the continued 'national awakening' brought the efforts of **FR Kreutzwald** to preserve the country's rich folk culture and the native language poems and plays of **Lydia Koidula** to the fore.

More recently, **Jann Kross's** Nobel Prize-nominated novels have catered to a growing post-independence desire to discover the national heritage through literature. The visual arts, comprising the work of domestic and foreign artists, are showcased in venues like the grand **Kadriorg Palace** (*see* pages 30–31) and the **National Library of Estonia**.

Architecture
UNESCO World Heritage

Tallinn's historic quarter is home to numerous fascinating and incredibly well-preserved old buildings, covering both **Medieval** and **Baroque** styles. Its role as the capital of the Estonian Soviet Socialist Republic (SSR), during five decades of 20th-century Russian rule, has played an important role in preserving Tallinn's architectural treasures, and some of the Old Town's original 13th-century buildings are still intact. The city's distinctive medieval appearance – complete with grand merchant houses, cobbled streets and vaulting church spires – which impresses visitors today was shaped by Tallinn's majority German population and its 16th-century Swedish rulers. Now protected as a UNESCO World Heritage Site, Vanalinn's longevity is assured.

Opposite: *St Olaf's, just one of many church spires in Tallinn's Old Town.*
Below: *An interesting dragon head water spout detail in the Old Town.*

Russian Influence

Centuries of Russian rule have also left an indelible mark on Tallinn, with many of the Baroque and Classical buildings that you will find in the city dating from the 17th to the 19th centuries. The post-World War II Soviet occupation of Estonia heralded bleaker times, in terms of architecture, for the capital. An influx of Russian workers was accompanied by the rapid construction of dense and character-less grey concrete **housing blocks**. Fortunately these are on the fringes of the Old Town, and, while they may be integral to Tallinn's history, few tourists ever really see them.

Glass and Steel

Tallinn is also currently undergoing something of a transformation, with many Soviet-era buildings being cleared to make way for gleaming new glass-and-steel constructions. The capital's penchant for **modern skyscrapers** is not just the result of market forces, and a significant element of symbolism is attached to the ongoing construction of dazzling office blocks and towering hotels. On one level Tallinn simply wants to show the rest of the world that Estonia is a prosperous and forward-thinking country where capitalist values thrive.

Contrasting Views

To really appreciate the contrast between old and new Tallinn you need to get up high. One good vantage point is the tower of **St Olaf's Church** (see pages 21–22). Looking southeast from the viewing platform you can see the terracotta rooftops of the Old Town give way to the big shiny high-rises of the business district beyond.

> **The Riot Act**
> On Friday 27 April 2007 Tallinn city authorities made the decision to remove the **Bronze Soldier**, a controversial Soviet war memorial that had stood outside the National Library since 1947. Seeing it as yet another infringement on their rights and a condemnation of their culture, more than 1000 of Tallinn's Russian residents took to the streets in a night of violent rioting. Sadly 153 people were injured and one died. A further 800 people were arrested. Skirmishes continued over the next few days before finally dying down.

⭐ *See Map A–B2* | ★★★

Tallinn Card
Valid for 24, 48 or 72 hours, the Tallinn Card is a useful discount card which entitles the holder to free public transport and a complimentary sightseeing tour (walking, by bus or by bicycle). It also offers free or discounted entrance to the majority of the city's museums, as well as discounts at spas, leisure facilities, restaurants and shops. Cards for the under-16s are half price. For those on a short visit the six-hour card provides some of the same benefits.

VANALINN

A UNESCO World Heritage Site, Tallinn's Vanalinn (Old Town) is effectively the Estonian capital's main attraction. This compact oasis began life as a small 9th-century settlement located on Toompea Hill. As Tallinn's Old Town gradually expanded it stretched out across the Lower Town (once an autonomous settlement) towards the Baltic Sea and later became encircled by sturdy medieval walls and fortifications. Much of Vanalinn's historic core today dates from as far back as the 13th century, and this chocolate box pretty Old Town is one of the most striking in Europe.

For locals and tourists alike, one of the biggest joys of spending time in Vanalinn comes from ambling along winding cobbled streets, sipping rich coffee in a pavement café, supping an Estonian beer, or simply sitting back and watching the stir of daily life. In addition, Tallinn's Old Town is crammed with historic buildings – many of which are open to the public – including old churches and opulent merchant houses. The capital also boasts first-rate restaurants and boutique shops that sell just about everything, from hand-knitted woollen clothing to exquisite amber jewellery and clothing fashioned by celebrated Estonian fashion designers.

Below: *Café culture is alive and well in modern-day Tallinn.*

RAEKOJA PLATS

Raekoja plats (Town Hall Square), the expansive plaza at the nucleus of Tallinn's Old

VANALINN & RAEKOJA PLATS

See Map A–C3	★★★

Town, is the place to come and watch local life bustle past. The attractive cobbled square, fringed by graceful buildings, has been at the heart of the city for eight centuries. Over the years it has served as a place for public executions, mass celebrations and even hosted a medieval marketplace. Today you are more likely to see a wedding party or, on a balmy summer's evening, catch an alfresco concert. During the main tourist season a number of craftspeople also peddle their wares on Raekoja plats. In December an oversized Christmas tree and a festive market bring seasonal cheer to this lively central space.

Above: *The tall spire of Tallinna raekoda, or Tallinn Town Hall, is topped by a weather vane.*

The centrepiece of Tallinn's Town Hall Square is the late-Gothic **Tallinna raekoda** (Tallinn Town Hall) whose spire stretches high above the cobbles. A civic building has stood on this spot since 1341, though most of the present structure dates from the early 15th century. The second floor tends to be used exclusively for private functions, but the general public can visit the exhibition hall in the three-nave cellar.

One striking feature of this handsome Gothic building is its weather vane. Constructed in 1530 and known locally as **Vana Toomas** (Old Thomas), it has been helping locals predict the weather for almost 500 years.

A colourful local legend surrounds Old Thomas. As a young man he reputedly beat the wealthy contenders (Thomas was poor)

Tallinna Raekoda
✉ Raekoja plats 1
☎ 645 7900
🖥 www.tallinn.ee/raekoda
🕐 **Town Hall** open 10:00–16:00 Tue–Sat, closed Sun & Mon (Jul–Aug), by appointment (Sep–Jun)
🕐 **Town Hall Exhibition** open 10:00–16:00 Tue–Sat, closed Sun & Mon (mid-May to mid-Oct), 11:00–17:00 Sat & Sun (mid-Oct to mid-May)

See Map A–B2   ★ ★ ★

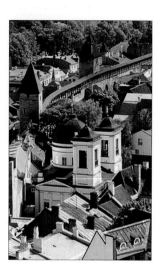

Above: *The city walls of Tallinn once boasted a total of 46 defence towers.*

in a shooting competition, felling the target bird with his first shot while the others failed to hit it at all. Apparently the Alderman of the Great Guild was so impressed that he trained Thomas as a town guardian.

The triumph of the underdog was such a popular story with locals that they adopted Old Thomas as an unofficial symbol of Tallinn. Not only is Old Thomas immortalized atop the Town Hall, you can also find his statue in the **Tallinn City Museum** (*see page 20*).

Incidentally, the original weather vane was destroyed during World War II. Today's incarnation of the fabled hero is a 1996 replica, which itself replaced a 1952 reconstruction.

A visit to the **Raeapteek** (Town Hall Pharmacy), one of the oldest operational pharmacies in Europe, whisks you back around 600 years. Today the medicine dispensed may be modern, but the interior has been kept as original as possible. One medicinal relic that tourists are welcome to try is the spiced claret wine that was widely believed to aid digestion and to cure a variety of ailments, including the plague.

MEDIEVAL FORTIFICATIONS

At the extremities of the Old Town you will come across a collection of literally unmissable fortifications. The thick walls and towers that were built around Vanalinn in the late 13th and early 14th centuries were gradually

Raeapteek
✉ Raekoja plats 11
☎ 631 4860
🕒 daily 10:00–18:00

Nunnatorn, Saunatorn un Kuldjalatorn
✉ Access via Suurkloostri
🕒 13:00–18:00
Tue–Fri, 10:00–14:00
Sat, closed Sun & Mon

See Map A–B4   ★ ★ ★

Kiek in de Kök
✉ Komandandi 2
☎ 644 6686
💻 www.linnamuuseum.ee/kiedindekok
🕐 10:30–17:00 Tue–Sun, closed Mon (Nov–Feb), 10:30–18:00 Tue–Sun, closed Mon (Mar–Oct)

expanded upon, and by the 16th century the Estonian capital boasted an enviable defence system. Back then the sturdy town wall was 3m (10ft) thick, stood 16m (52ft) high and stretched 4km (2.5 miles) around the Old City. It also boasted a phenomenal 46 defence towers. Just over half of this (2km/1.2 miles of wall and 26 towers) still stands today. Most of the towers are inaccessible to the public, with the exception of the neighbouring Nunnery, Sauna and Kuldjala towers.

If you want to climb on to Tallinn's Old City walls, go to the **Nunnatorn** (Nunnery Tower). From here you can take the steps up onto the wall and walk along a wooden balcony to the **Saunatorn** (Sauna Tower) and the **Kuldjalatorn** (Kuldjala Tower).

KIEK IN DE KÖK

Situated on Toompea Hill (*see* page 24) **Kiek in de kök** (Peek in the Kitchen) is an imposing 15th-century cannon tower. Upon completion the fortress boasted 4m (13ft) thick walls, a diameter of 17m (56ft) and stood 38m (125ft) tall. Its unusual name arose because the guard could see into neighbouring kitchens. The real advantage of this was that if they could look down into nearby properties the lookout could easily see what the enemy was doing below.

Superior in its firepower to Vanalinn's other fortifications, Kiek in de kök accommodated 27 cannons and 30 handguns in its embrasures. By 1760 the tower had become redundant (in a military capacity) and was

Below: *Kiek in de kök tower was once a very important part of Tallinn's fortifications.*

See Map A | ★★★

Above: *A depiction of a medieval merchant's house on display at the Tallinn City Museum.*

later used for storing state archives and residential accommodation instead.

Today the tower, which has been reconstructed at various intervals (most recently in 1968), houses the branch of the **Tallinn City Museum** (*see page 20*) that documents the city's military history. Artefacts on display include those from the Livonian War. Highlights for visitors are the opportunity to go inside this medieval fortification, the replica guns and cannons on display, the scale model of Tallinn in 1683 and the Old Town views from the embrasures.

BASTIONIDE KÄIGUD

In 2007 a 380m (1247ft) long stretch of the **Bastionide käigud** (Secret Tunnels) that lie beneath Tallinn's Old City walls was opened to the public. Admission is currently by guided tour only, with groups meeting at Kiek in de kök.

Dating from the 17th and 18th centuries, these hidden limestone passages were designed to shelter the soldiers manning the defensive towers and to allow undetected movement between them. At their broadest points the tunnels measure 1.5m (5ft) wide and 3m (10ft) high. The skills learned for use in the tunnels were never really put into practice, and in the 18th century the subterranean chambers were gradually turned into storerooms. During World War II they served as air-raid shelters.

Bastionide Käigud
⊠ Komandandi 2
☎ 644 6686
🖳 www.linnamuuseum.ee/kiedindekok
🕐 open for guided tours

⭐ *See* Map A–D1   ★ ★ ★

SUUR RANNAVÄRAV UN PAKS MARGAREETA

North of the Old Town, **Suur rannavärav** (Great Coastal Gate) and **Paks Margareeta** (Fat Margaret's Tower) were constructed close to Tallinn Harbour to protect Vanalinn against attack from the sea. In the early 16th century, the gate was designed to provide both a grand entrance to the city and, through the addition of the round cannon tower, to ward off unwanted visitors.

Standing just 22m (72ft) tall and with a girth of 25m (82ft), Fat Margaret's was (and still is) the stoutest tower in Vanalinn's defensive system. At their broadest point its grey brick walls are 5.5m (18ft) thick. As the threat of attack dwindled the tower became a munitions store. It also served as a prison between 1830 and 1917.

Today the defunct fortification houses the **Eesti meremuuseum** (Estonian Maritime Museum), worth visiting for the elevated views over the bay and back to the Old Town alone. The museum also exhibits seafaring paraphernalia from around the country, shedding light on Estonia's maritime history, its shipbuilding heritage and its major ports. Photographs and artefacts also look at anchors, diving equipment, lighthouses and navigational tools. Temporary exhibitions grace the ground floor.

Two of Tallinn's other ancient portals, the **Viru väravad** (Viru Gates), delineate the eastern entrance to the Old Town. Like all of Vanalinn's circular towers,

Paks Margareeta/ Eesti Meremuuseum
✉ Pikk 70
☎ 641 1408
🖥 www.mere muuseum.ee
🕐 10:00–18:00 Wed–Sun, closed Mon & Tue. Fat Margaret's may well be Tallinn's fattest medieval guard tower; however (contrary to popular belief), its name didn't come from its stocky appearance but from one of the thickset cannons that was used to defend the tower.

Below: *Fat Margaret's Tower, once integral to the city's defences, is now a tourist attraction.*

HIGHLIGHTS

🌀 See Map A–C2 ★★★

Above: *Viru Gates mark the eastern entrance into the Old Town.*

these 14th-century turrets are capped with a red conical roof and look as if they have been transported straight from the pages of a fairytale. Photography is not the only reason to seek out this attractive spot, as some of the best handmade linen and knitted garments are sold in the **Knit Market** (*see* page 52) located close to the portal.

TALLINNA LINNAMUUSEUM

Anyone who wants to learn more about Tallinn's fascinating history should make a beeline for **Tallinna linnamuuseum** (Tallinn City Museum). Here you can trace the capital's evolution from medieval times through to its 1991 independence. Since it opened in 1937 the museum's collection has swollen to more than 150,000 items and includes old tools, weapons, jewellery, textiles and decorative leather, as well as ornamental glass, coins, medals, period furniture, antique vases, ceramics and stone carvings. Its fascinating photographic archives include images shot during both the Soviet and German occupations of Tallinn.

MUSTPEADE MAJA

The **Mustpeade maja** (House of the Brotherhood of Blackheads) guild house is one of the few **Renaissance** buildings still standing in Tallinn today. Membership to the **Brotherhood of the Blackheads** (an organization that dates from 1399) was

---

Kissing Hill
This small area of greenery is located just inside the **Viru Gates** (close to McDonald's) and up a small flight of steps. The pleasant Old Town setting, trees and shrubs may make a reasonably romantic setting, but it is hardly secluded and the presence of other tourists and local youths might put you off smooching despite the 'hill's' amorous name. It might not be the best spot for a kiss, but Kissing Hill does let you spy on passers-by.

MUSTPEADE MAJA & OLEVISTE KIRIK

☀ *See* Map A–D1	★ ★ ★

seen as a stepping stone to joining the **Great Guild** (*see* page 35). Unlike its bigger sibling, this mercantile club also accepted foreign members.

The exterior, which features intricate carvings, dates from the 16th century and its colourful door from 1640. The neoclassical interior is the result of a 1908 makeover. If you want to get inside ask the local tourist office if there are any classical music concerts scheduled during your visit. Alternatively, visit the property's website, where forthcoming events are listed (currently in Estonian only). On concert nights the box office opens an hour before the performance begins.

Tallinna Linnamuuseum
✉ Vene 17
☎ 644 6553
🖳 www.linna muuseum.ee
🕐 10:30–17:00 Wed–Mon, closed Tue (Nov–Feb); 10:30–18:00 Wed–Mon, closed Tue (Mar–Oct)

Mustpeade Maja
✉ Pikk 26
☎ 631 3199
🖳 www.mustpeade maja.ee
🕐 open for concerts and private functions

OLEVISTE KIRIK

When it was consecrated in the late 13th century its 140m (259ft) steeple made **Oleviste kirik** (St Olaf's Church) one of the tallest buildings in Europe. According to the city authorities it was actually the world's highest building in the year 1500, when its tower stood 159m (522ft) tall.

Today the steeple (a 19th-century replacement) stretches up a mere 120m (394ft); it is a minnow when it comes to world architecture. However, this attractive Baptist church is still a main feature of the Tallinn skyline.

Below: *The colourful 1640 door of the House of the Brotherhood of Blackheads.*

9/2164757

HIGHLIGHTS

Oleviste Kirik
✉ Pikk 48
☎ 641 2241
🖥 www.oleviste.ee
🕐 10:00–14:00 daily
and also during church
services

See Map A–B4 | ★★★

Although the church owes its name to **King
Olaf II of Norway**, to whom it is dedicated, an
alternative explanation exists in local folklore. This version claims that the church was
built by an unfortunate man, called Olaf,
who plummeted to his death while working
on the tower. A snake is said to have slithered
and a toad hopped from Olaf's mouth when
he landed. It seems that the church itself is as
unlucky as Olaf, as its steeple has been struck
by lightning eight times and the whole building razed by fire at least three times.

NIGULISTE KIRIK

Championed as one of the best examples of
Medieval architecture in Estonia, the original **Niguliste kirik** (St Nicholas's Church)
was built in the early 13th century. Much of
what you see today, however, is the result
of 15th, 18th and 20th-century modifica-
tions, the latter after the church was dam-
aged by Soviet bombs in World War II.
Dedicated to the patron saint of sailors and
fishermen, it was built before the Old Town
walls and originally had both
an ecclesiastical and a defensive role. When it was first
opened it had heavy bars
across its doors and windows.
These were removed when
the old city fortifications were
completed.

Like many of Tallinn's places
of worship, St Nicholas's doesn't
just have a spiritual role today.
After renovations were complete in the 1980s it became

Opposite: *The con-
trasting spires of
the Church of the
Holy Spirit and St
Olaf's Church.*
Below: *The elegant
medieval paintings
on display are one
of the attractions in
St Nicholas's Church.*

☆ *See* Map A–C3

★★★

home to an art museum. It is also a popular concert venue.

The **artistic treasures** displayed inside the church include intricate carvings, ornate chandeliers, a late 15th-century high altar and the 16th-century altar of St Anthony (which miraculously survived the fire that engulfed the church after the 1944 bombing). Considered even more important is an early section of Bernt Notke's *Danse Macabre*.

PÜHAVAIMU KIRIK

The humble 14th-century **Pühavaimu kirik** (Church of the Holy Spirit) is significant for a number of reasons, including the fact that it is one of the oldest religious buildings in Tallinn. Perhaps more important was the role that it played in the promotion of the **Estonian language**, with services held in the native tongue and former pastor, **Johann Koell**, credited as the author of the first book published in Estonian, *Catechism*, in 1535. Intricate wooden carvings combine to create a striking interior, while the late 15th-century altar, the work of **Berndt Notke**, is considered one of the most valuable medieval sculptures in the country. Also noteworthy is the church clock (dating from the 17th century), Tallinn's oldest surviving public timepiece.

DOMINIIKLASTE KLOOSTRI MUUSEUM

Dating from 1246 **St Catherine's Dominican Monastery** is the oldest preserved building in Vanalinn. More than just a place of worship,

Niguliste Kirik
✉ Niguliste 3
☎ 631 4330
🖥 www.ekm.ee
🕐 10:00–17:00 Wed–Sun, closed Mon & Tue. In the winter months a section of Harju Street (outside the church) is transformed into an outdoor ice-skating rink known as **Uisuplats** (or the Skating Place). The rink is open 10:00–22:00 every day and also has a café.

Pühavaimu Kirik
✉ Pühavaimu 2
☎ 646 4430
🖥 www.eelk.ee/tallinna.puhavaimu
🕐 09:30–17:30 Mon–Sat, 10:00–16:00 Sun (Jan–Apr); 09:30–18:30 Mon–Sat, 10:00–18:30 Sun (May–Aug); 10:00–17:30 daily (Sep–Dec)

Above: *The arched doorway of St Catherine's Dominican Monastery is in the Gothic style.*

⊛ *See* Map A–D4 ★★

the monastery has also functioned as a school. Today it is home to the **Dominiiklaste kloostri muuseum** (Dominican Monastery Museum), which is worth visiting to see its handsome Gothic appearance, to learn more about the Dominicans in Tallinn and to admire its ornate cloisters and extensive collection of carved stone.

The monastery has not survived eight centuries unscathed, falling victim to fire in 1531, after which it was only partially restored. Other parts of the complex, like the north tower church bells, are later additions.

The monastery once contained three residential wings, which together comprised the **Dominiiklaste kloostri klausuuris** (Dominican Monastery Cloister). Today just one wing, the east wing, remains. A tour of the dormitory, library, refectory and the prior's living quarters give an intriguing insight into the lifestyle of medieval monks. The old vestry is given over to an art exhibition.

Dominiiklaste Kloostri Muuseum
✉ Vene 16/18
☎ 644 4606
🖥 www.kloostri.ee
🕐 10:00–18:00 daily (mid-May to late Sep), by appointment (late Sep to mid-May)

Dominiiklaste Kloostri Klausuuris
✉ Müürivahe 33
☎ 644 6530
🕐 10:00–17:00 daily (mid-May to Aug), closed Sep to early May (booking essential)

TOOMPEA

The short but steep ascent up Toompea (Cathedral Hill) more than rewards the effort. Highlights up here include **Toompea loss** (Toompea Castle) and the **Aleksander Nevski katedraal** (Alexander Nevsky Cathedral). Most visitors climb Toompea, however, for the sweeping views back across Tallinn and out to the Baltic Sea. This dramatic vista can best be appreciated from one of two viewing platforms.

As the place where the Danes laid the foundations of modern-day Tallinn, Toompea has a special place in the heart of many

TOOMPEA

See Map A–A3 & A4   ★★

Estonians. It is easy to see why the Danish crusaders chose this spot, as the limestone hill at the centre of Vanalinn stands 20–30m (66–98ft) higher than the rest of the city. Few people realize that for much of its history Toompea was actually a separate town and was only united with the Lower Town in 1878.

More than just the geographical heart of Tallinn's Old Town, Toompea is the centre of Estonian power, with the parliament and other government offices located here.

Toompea Loss

Home to the **Riigikogu** (Estonian Parliament), the 13th-century **Toompea loss** (Toompea Castle) has become a poignant symbol of Estonian national identity and power. A fortress has stood on this spot since it was occupied by early traders who constructed a wooden fort here back in the 9th century. When the Danes took over the territory in 1219 they razed the original structure and replaced it with a sturdy stone castle, parts of which still remain today. Since then Toompea Castle has been at the centre of government, with Tallinn's German, Swedish and Russian occupiers ruling Estonia from here. An iconic structure, the castle stands 50m (164ft) above sea level. One of the most impressive parts of the complex is the **Pikk Hermann** (Tall Hermann's Tower). Forming the south-western corner of the fortress and standing approximately

Danish King's Garden
One of the most underrated attractions on Toompea Hill is the Danish King's Garden, a small leafy park that overloooks St Nicholas's Church. As you enter the tranquil park, look out for a shield bearing the Danish flag. Like many things in Tallinn this is steeped in local folklore. Apparently the Danes, on the verge of defeat, asked God to help; in return he gave them their national flag. To reach the garden follow Lühike jalg from St Nicholas's Church and keep your eyes peeled for the park's gates, which are located on the left.

Below: *Toompea Castle, seat of the Estonian Parliament.*

Aleksander Nevski Katedraal
✉ Lossi plats 10
☎ 644 3484
🕐 open 08:00–19:00 daily, services 08:30 and 17:00 daily

⭐ *See* Map A–B4   ★★

48m (157ft) high, the tower is a 14th-century addition. Its namesake, Hermann, was a medieval hero who died fighting for the Teutonic Knights. Today Pikk Hermann proudly flies the Estonian flag.

Since regaining its independence in 1991 Estonia fittingly continues to be ruled from this spot, although not from the castle itself but from the parliament building that stands in the courtyard. This colourful pink structure dates from the 1920s and Estonia's first spell as an autonomous State.

ALEKSANDER NEVSKI KATEDRAAL

Opposite: *The spire of the Dome Church (Toomkirik), which claims to be the oldest in Estonia.*
Below: *Alexander Nevsky Cathedral has distinctive black onion domes in the Russian Revival style.*

The Orthodox **Aleksander Nevski katedraal** (Alexander Nevsky Cathedral), completed in 1900, was constructed at the behest of Tsar Alexander III. Designed by **Mikhail Preobrazhensky** and built in a Russian Revival style, the church boasts striking black onion domes and is arguably the most attractive house of prayer in Tallinn. Its physical attributes include the largest cupola in the city and the biggest bell. Weighing in at 15,000kg (15 tonnes), the enormous bell is one of 11 that ring out as a reminder that a service is imminent.

The cathedral has apparently suffered from a number of structural problems, which locals claim have occurred because although it was built in honour of a Russian hero it is, somewhat erroneously, located on the grave of an Estonian one. The cathedral's namesake, St Alexander Nevsky, is famous among the Russian community for his victory over the

See Map A–B3 ★★

Teutonic Knights in the Battle on the Ice, which took place on **Lake Peipsi** (Peipsi järv) in 1242. This defeat of the Baltic German knights was celebrated as an act that saved Russia from domination by the West and resulted in Nevsky's canonization by the Russian Orthodox Church. The hero in this story is **Kalevipoeg**, son of the giant Kalev, who became synonymous in folklore with the liberation of Estonia. Toompea is just one of the places that the legendary Kalevipoeg is supposed to be buried.

Tall stories aside, the building stirs up complex issues for Tallinn's residents. Despised as a symbol of hundreds of years of Russian oppression by many Estonians, plans were mooted for the church's demolition back in 1924. Fortunately this never happened and despite ambivalent attitudes towards the cathedral, this architectural gem has been restored in recent years.

TOOMKIRIK

When the Danes settled on Toompea Hill in 1219, they also commissioned the city's first church, albeit a temporary wooden structure. With its origins rooted in the early 13th century, the **Toomkirik** (Dome Church), somewhat confusingly also known as **The Cathedral of St Mary the Virgin** or **St Mary's**, claims to be the oldest in Estonia.

Although work on the replacement stone structure began in 1229, the building that stands today has changed dramatically over the years. Its attractive Gothic façade dates from the 14th century, but much of the exterior and interior were reconstructed

Toomkirik
✉ Toom-Kooli 6
☎ 644 4140
🖳 www.eelk.ee/tallinna.toom
🕓 09:00–17:00 Tue–Sun, closed Mon. Services are held at 10:00 on Sundays, with an Estonian-only service held on the third Sunday of the month. Organ concerts are held at 12:00 on Saturdays and this is a particularly good time to visit the church. Be considerate of Tallinn's Lutheran congregation and don't visit during services unless you want to attend one. Incidentally, until the 16th-century Protestant Reformation the Cathedral was actually Catholic, converting to Lutheranism in 1561.

See Map A–B5 ★

Above: *A Sputnik and a collection of prison cell doors on display at the Occupation Museum.*

after fire ravaged Toompea in 1684.

A striking Baroque pulpit, shields sporting the coats of arms of Tallinn's 17th–20th-century aristocracy and 13th–18th-century graves of influential residents of yesteryear reward those who venture inside. Look out for **Otto Johann Thuve's** tombstone. In life Thuve loved parties, wine and women; seeking redemption in death he requested that his grave be placed where the devout could kneel and pray as they entered the church.

OKUPATSIOONIDE MUUSEUM

Toompea Street (not the hill itself) is home to the **Okupatsioonide muuseum** (Occupation Museum), whose permanent collection sheds light on life in an occupied Estonia between 1940 and 1991. Its sobering artefacts hark back to the bleak periods of both Soviet and Nazi occupation of Tallinn, and Estonia as a whole. The most compelling components of the collection regarding Soviet rule include eyewitness accounts captured on film, shabby prison uniforms, photographs, replica trains (to symbolize the mass deportations) and sections dedicated to the desperate flight of thousands of refugees. Meanwhile, the illustration of the fate of the Estonian Jews at the hands of the Nazis is equally moving.

Almost as interesting as the museum

Okupatsioonide Muuseum
✉ Toompea 8
☎ 668 0250
🖳 www.okupatsioon.ee
🕑 11:00–18:00 Tue–Sun, closed Mon

See Map A–D1	★

itself is the fact that it was funded at a cost of $2 million (about 1.4 million euros) by an Estonian expatriate called **Olga Ritso**. Ritso's experiences as a young woman – her father was a victim of the Soviet deportations to Siberia (in total around 35,000 Estonians were banished) when she was just two years old and her uncle when she was 20 – motivated her to donate the money.

ESTONIAN FERRY MONUMENT

North of the Old Town, close to Tallinn's port, the Estonian Ferry Monument is one of the capital's most poignant sights and an enduring reminder of the 1994 ferry disaster. In the early hours of the morning of 28 September that year the Stockholm-bound *MS Estonia* sank in the pitch dark Baltic Sea, plunging 852 passengers and crew (mainly Swedes and Estonians) to their deaths. Only 137 people were lucky enough to survive.

The investigation that followed looked at the weather conditions (the sea was rough but not unusually so for the time of year), the speed of the ferry, power failure and problems with communications equipment. Eventually the tragedy was blamed on a poorly designed bow door (though local rumours have spawned various conspiracy theories) and as water rushed on to the car deck the ship listed dangerously, making moving around almost impossible. Though the first rescue craft arrived within an hour of receiving the mayday call, for many this was already too late. Sadly for the relatives of those who died only 10% of the bodies of the deceased were ever recovered.

Bird's-eye View
Various places in central Tallinn boast stunning Old and New Town views. Admire the views over the Old Town and port as you dance the night away at **Panoraam** (Mere pst 8b). Alternatively, dine in **Margarita** (Suur-Karja 7), or take in the skyline from **Lounge 24** (Radisson SAS, Rävala 3). Enjoy the panorama for free from the viewing platforms on **Kohtuotsa** and **Patkuli**, or climb the spire of **St Olaf's Church** (*see* page 21). Get even higher and soak up the view from the **TV Tower** (*see* page 31). Another great panorama is available from the rooftop terrace at the **Estonian Maritime Museum** (*see* page 19).

See Maps A–E2 & B–H3 ★

Eesti Arhitektuuri-muuseum

✉ Ahtri 2
☎ 625 7000
🖥 www.arhitektuuri
muuseum.ee
🕐 12:00–20:00 Wed–
Fri, 11:00–18:00 Sat &
Sun, closed Mon & Tue
(mid-May to Sep);
11:00–18:00 Wed–Sun,
closed Mon & Tue (Oct
to mid-May)
🛈 free admission on
the last Friday of the
month

Kadrioru Loss

✉ Weizenbergi 37
☎ 606 6400
🖥 www.ekm.ee
🕐 10:00–17:00 Tue–
Sun, closed Mon (May–
Sep); 10:00–17:00
Wed–Sun, closed Mon
(Oct–Apr)

The memorial itself, a large curved line made from stone with a big chunk cut out of the middle, is simple and striking. The missing segment of the *Broken Line*, as it is called, pays tribute to those who lost their lives.

EESTI ARHITEKTUURIMUUSEUM

To learn more about Tallinn's rich architectural heritage, or to see temporary exhibitions dedicated to triumphs and tragedies in building design from around the globe, head to the **Eesti arhitektuurimuuseum** (Estonian Architecture Museum). Highlights in a permanent collection that runs to 7000 pieces include photos, town plans, maps, scale drawings and models, as well as templates for post-World War II victory monuments and concrete housing blocks.

The building that houses the museum, **Rottermann's Salt Storage House**, is worth visiting in its own right. This Baltic-German limestone warehouse near the harbour is a striking industrial building dating from 1908.

KADRIORU LOSS

Below: *Kadriorg Palace on the outskirts of the city is one of the most elegant buildings in Tallinn.*

A handful of attractions are clustered in Tallinn's northeastern suburbs. Of these, **Kadrioru loss** (Kadriorg Palace), commissioned by Peter the Great in 1718 in an extravagant display of affection for his wife Catherine, is the most impressive. The

⚜ *See* Map C–G2 | ★

graceful Baroque building was modelled on lavish Italian villas and was the result of the blood, sweat and tears of craftsmen from Russia, Italy, Sweden and Latvia.

As Estonia embarked upon its first period of independence, the palace became home to the **Eesti kunstimuuseum** (Estonian Art Museum) in 1921. After 1929 the exhibits became mobile again – as Kadriorg became the residence of the Estonian president – and didn't return to the palace until 1946.

By the time the Soviets moved out of Tallinn in 1991 the building had become so dilapidated that it was closed for almost a decade for extensive renovation. The present **Kadrioru kunstimuuseum** (Kadriorg Art Museum) reopened, as one of five branches of the Estonian Art Museum, in 2000. It exhibits paintings by Russian and European artists from the 16th to the 20th century.

The palace is worth visiting just to stroll around the elegant grounds of Kadriorg Park. This beauty spot comprises a lake, woodland, formal gardens and meadows.

TALLINNA TELETORN

It may be a bit of an eyesore, but the **Tallinna teletorn** (Tallinn TV Tower) has some redeeming features. First are the far-reaching views from the 170m (558ft) viewing platform. On a clear day these stretch out across the Baltic Sea to Finland and back to the Old Town. Opened in 1980, the tower actually stands 314m (1030ft) high.

Have a meal in the bar-restaurant – a bit of a surreal experience as the whole place seems to be stuck in a 1980s timewarp.

Tallinna Teletorn
⊠ Kloostrimetsa 58a
🕐 10:00–24:00 daily.
According to local reports the TV Tower was the target of Soviet resistance to Estonia's declaration of independence on 20 August 1991. Apparently Soviet troops attempted to storm the television station the following day, but were unsuccessful, as locals had already gathered to form pre-emptive human barricades around stations broadcasting TV and radio programmes.

Places of Worship

Aleksander Nevski Katedraal (Alexander Nevsky Cathedral)

For information *see* pages 26–27.

✉ *Lossi plats 10,* ☎ *644 3484,* ◷ *08:00– 19:00 daily. Services 08:30 & 17:00 daily.*

Jewish Synagogue

Estonia was the first of the three Baltic States to be declared 'free of Jews' *(Judenfrei)* by the Nazis during World War II. This declaration was made after around three-quarters of the country's Jewish population had fled to the Soviet Union. Most of the rest had been shipped off to concentration camps (where the majority later died) and bombs had obliterated synagogues in Tallinn and Tartu. The end of the war did not stop the persecution, with those Estonian and Russian Jews who dared return to the city prohibited from overtly practising Judaism and being forced to meet in secret. Estonian independence in 1991 restored religious freedom and the capital now has an Estonian Jewish Cultural Centre whose key components include a synagogue (opened in 2000), Jewish school, Jewish Museum and a kosher restaurant.

✉ *Karu 16,* ☎ *662 3050,* ⬛ *www.ejc.ee* ◷ *10:00–18:00 Mon– Thu, 10:00–14:00 Fri (Oct–Apr); 10:00–18:00 Mon–Thu, 10:00–17:00 Fri (May–Sep). Services at 10:00 Mon–Thu, 14:15 daily, 08:15 Wed, 07:00 Fri, 10:00 Sat (Shabbat/Sabbath).*

Kaasani Jumalaema Sündimise Kirik

Located just south of Vanalinn the Kaasani jumalaema sündimise kirik (Church of Our Lady of Kazan) is the oldest timber building still standing in Tallinn today. This small

Orthodox church was constructed in 1721 and any restoration work over the years has been sympathetic to the original structure. Its most striking aspects are its cross shape and Classicist interior.

☒ *Liivalaia 38,*
☎ *660 6373,*
🕑 *08:00–14:00 daily. Services at 08:00, 11:00 & 16:30 Sat & Sun (in Russian).*

Oleviste Kirik (St Olaf's Church)

For information *see* page 21.

☒ *Pikk 48,*
☎ *641 2241,*
💻 *www.oleviste.ee*
🕑 *10:00–14:00 daily and during church services.*

Püha Nikolai Imetegija Kirik

Although a Russian Orthodox church has stood on Vene (which translates as Russian Street) since the beginning of the 15th century, today's Püha Nikolai imetegija kirik (St Nicholas's Orthodox Church) was built in the 1820s. Historically, this neoclassical gem was at the heart of the medieval marketplace frequented by Tallinn's Russian tradesmen. Amongst the various icons on display inside the church the most valuable is the iconostasis (the icon-adorned screen which separates the nave from the sanctuary).

☒ *Vene 24,* ☎ *644 1945,* 🕑 *10:00–18:00 Mon–Fri, 08:00–21:00 Sat, 07:30–15:00 Sun. Services at 18:00 Fri, 09:00 & 18:00 Sat, 10:00 Sun.*

Niguliste Kirik (St Nicholas's Church)

For information *see* pages 22–23.

☒ *Niguliste 3,* ☎ *631 4330,* 💻 *www.ekm.ee* 🕑 *10:00–17:00 Wed– Sun, closed Mon & Tue.*

Jaani Kirik

Jaani kirik (St John's Church) is an Evangelical-Lutheran church. Construction work began in 1862

Opposite: *The Church of Our Lady of Kazan is the oldest wooden building in Tallinn.*

Estonia's Jews
Before the World War II Nazi occupation of Estonia there were around 4000 Jews living in the country, mainly in Tallinn. Fortunately around 75% managed to escape to Russia, but of the 1000 or so that remained the majority had fallen victim to the Holocaust by the end of 1941. Estonian Jews also suffered at the hands of the Russians, with businesses nationalized, schools, synagogues and other Jewish institutions closed and the practice of Judaism banned. The question of how complicit some Estonians were in the rounding up and murder of their fellow countrymen remains a source of some debate.

Above: *Detail of a mural in the Great Guild Hall.*

(taking five years in total) as a direct response to the need for a larger place of worship than the Church of the Holy Spirit (see page 23), whose congregation (somewhere in the region of 14,000 people) was simply too big to fit inside. This yellow landmark is located just south of the Old City walls and is the work of Tallinn-born architect Christoph August Gabler (1820–84), with at least some of the funds for the work being raised by Tallinn's Lutheran community. This attractive neo-Gothic church is worth visiting to see the ornaments that have been donated to it over the years, including chandeliers and candelabras, as well as its neo-Gothic organ and attractive altarpiece. Seemingly incongruous amongst the functional architecture of Vabaduse väljak (Freedom Square), the church's fate has been on shaky ground at various intervals throughout its history: towards the end of the 1930s the local authorities made rumblings about pulling it down (World War II and the subsequent Soviet occupation of the city stopped this plan in its tracks), with demolition plans mooted again in the 1950s. ✉ *Vabaduse väljak 1,* ☎ *644 6206,* 🖥 *http:// jaani.eelk.ee* 🕒 *10:00– 14:00 Tue, Thu & Fri, 10:00–18:00 Wed. Service 10:00 Sun. Musical Prayer 13:30 Wed.*

Pühavaimu Kirik (Church of the Holy Spirit)

For information *see page 23.*
✉ *Pühavaimu 2,* ☎ *646 4430,* 🖥 *www. eelk.ee/tallinna. puhavaimu* 🕒 *09:30– 17:30 Mon–Sat, 10:00–16:00 Sun (Jan–Apr); 09:30–18:30 Mon–Sat, 10:00–18:30 Sun (May–Aug); 10:00–17:30 daily (Sep–Dec).*

HISTORIC BUILDINGS

Historic Buildings

Suurgildi Hoone

The Suurgildi hoone (Great Guild Hall), the former meeting place of Tallinn's wealthy merchants, dates from 1417. This grand building, beaten only by the Town Hall (excluding religious buildings) when it comes to size in the medieval city, was constructed as an ostentatious display of affluence and power. Both the exterior (look for the Great Guild's coat of arms) and interior largely retain their original appearance. It is home to the Old Town branch of the Eesti ajaloomuuseum (Estonian History Museum) where you can trace the country's development from early settlement to the 18th century. The coin room boasts a collection dedicated to currency that has been used in Estonia through the ages.
✉ Suurgildi hoone/ Eesti ajaloomuuseum Pikk 17, ☎ 641 1630,

🖥 www.eam.ee
🕐 11:00–18:00 Thu–Tue, closed Wed.
💰 Free admission on the last Saturday of the month.

Former KGB Headquarters

Home to the present-day Interior Ministry, the former KGB Headquarters on Pikk Street are not an official tourist sight as such. This building with bricked-up cellar windows is interesting nonetheless, as the place where misery was inflicted upon the countless dissidents facing deportation to Siberia. The basement housed the cells where the deportees were incarcerated prior to their journey. During Soviet times people joked that this must be the tallest building on the globe because it was possible to see Siberia from the cellar.
✉ Pikk 61.

Three Sisters

Three adjacent 14th-century merchant houses on Pikk Street rank amongst Vana-linn's most attractive. Almost identical in appearance, they have been dubbed the 'Three Sisters'. Today this trio of medieval buildings functions as an up-market hotel (see page 55). If you want a peek inside, then visit the hotel's wine bar or book a seat in its fine-dining restaurant.
✉ Pikk 71.

Maarjamäe War Memorial

The overblown obelisk situated on the Pirita Highway forms part of the larger Maarjamäe War Memorial complex, whose imposing concrete sculptures were typical of the 1950s and 60s. Dedicated to Soviet heroism, they are marked by triumphalist gestures. The vaulting spire commemorates the loss of Russian lives during World War I, while the iron and concrete statues commemorate

SIGHTSEEING

Below: *The Bronze Soldier statue is the most controversial monument in Tallinn today.*

Soviet bravery during World War II.
⊠ *Pirita Highway.*

The Bronze Soldier

A rare relic of communism, the Bronze Soldier, which was controversially located outside the National Library for 50 years, is another tribute to the bravery of Russian troops during World War II. Many locals saw it as a celebration of the postwar Soviet occupation of Estonia and repeatedly called for its removal. In 2007 the government finally ordered its relocation to Tallinna kaitseväe kalmistu (The Tallinn Defence Forces Cemetery or Tallinn Military Cemetery), a move that sparked rioting by the Russian community (*see panel, page 13*).
⊠ *Filtri 13,*
🖳 *www.kalmistud.ee*

Museums and Galleries
Mikkeli Muuseum

The private collection of Johannes Mikkel is housed in a former kitchen building at Kadriorg Palace (*see pages 30–31*). The Mikkeli muuseum (Mikkel Museum) may not be worth making the trip out of town for alone, but the gallery does have a decent collection of Dutch and Flemish paintings, as well as artefacts from around the globe.
⊠ *Weizenbergi 28,*
☎ *601 5844,* 🖳 *www. ekm.ee* 🕘 *11:00–17:00 Wed–Sun, closed Mon & Tue.*

Eduard Vilde Muuseum

Nearby, the Eduard Vilde muuseum (Eduard Vilde Museum) commemorates the life and writing of the renowned Estonian author. For non-Estonians the exhibition of contemporary art on display in the Kastellaani galerii (Kastellaani Gallery) may be of more interest.

✉ Roheline aas 3,
☎ 601 3181, 🖥 www.
linnamuuseum.ee
🕓 11:00–17:00 Wed–
Mon, closed Tue
(Nov–Jan); 11:00–
18:00 Wed–Mon,
closed Tue (Mar–Oct).

Tammsaare Muuseum

The life and work of
another famous Esto-
nian literary figure –
Anton Hansen
Tammsaare – is
commemorated just
off the main road
(Narva mnt) in the
Tammsaare muuseum
(Tammsaare Museum).
Tammsaare's seminal
work, *Truth and
Justice*, earned him
the reputation as the
country's best 20th-
century author. The
writer lived in the
apartment that is
now the museum
from 1932 until his
death in 1940.
✉ Koidula 12a,
☎ 601 3232, 🖥 www.
linnamuuseum.ee
🕓 10:00–17:00 Wed–
Mon, closed Tue.
💰 Free admission last
Friday of the month.

🚃 Koidula tram and
bus stop.

Eesti Ajaloomuuseum

Heading further east
along the coast brings
you to Maarjamäe
loss (Maarjamäe
Palace) and another
branch of the Eesti
ajaloomuuseum
(Estonian History
Museum), which
documents the
country's long and
difficult path to self-
government.
✉ Pirita tee 56,
☎ 622 8600,
🖥 www.eam.ee
🕓 11:00–18:00 Wed–
Sun, closed Mon &
Tue (Mar–Oct); 10:00–
17:00 Wed–Sun,
closed Mon & Tue
(Nov–Feb).
💰 Free admission on
the last Saturday of
the month.
🚃 Maarjamäe bus
stop.

Eesti Vabaõhumuuseum

Its pleasant woodland
location on the Bay of
Kopli is reason
enough to make the

Eduard Vilde

Eduard Vilde (1865–
1933) is commonly
regarded as one of
Estonia's best writers.
Early in his career Vilde
focused on travelogues,
embellishing his own
experiences with
imaginary people and
events. At the young
age of 17 he also
became a journalist
and went on to work
for various newspapers
during his lifetime. By
the beginning of the
20th century Vilde had
turned his hand to his-
torical novels, which,
like his travelogues,
seamlessly blended fact
and fiction. Vilde's most
famous book is *The
Milkman from Mäeküla*.

Anton Hansen Tammsaare

Frequently cited as
Estonia's most famous
literary son, Anton
Hansen Tammsaare
(1878–1940) moved to
Tallinn with his new
bride in September
1919. The author's
most celebrated work,
Truth and Justice,
examines man's rela-
tionship with the earth,
God, society, the self
and resignation over
five volumes. In life
Tammsaare battled with
ill health and the
demands of raising a
family, and it is widely
believed that his own
experiences provided the
basis for his characters.

Opposite: *Kumu Art Museum contains the work of many Estonian artists.*
Below: *The Estonian Open-air Museum is a recreation of 18th- to 20th-century rural Estonia.*

short trip out of town to the Eesti Vabaõhu-muuseum (Estonian Open-air Museum). Here you can travel back in time to 18th- to 20th-century rural Estonia and explore a dozen timber farm-steads. Some old mills, a traditional inn and a wooden schoolhouse are also among the 72 build-ings that form this recreated village.
✉ *Vabaõhumuuseemi 12,* ☎ *654 9100,* 🖥 *www.evm.ee* ⏱ *10:00–20:00 daily (Apr–Oct); 10:00–17:00 (Nov–Mar). In the winter months a lot of the farmhouses are closed so you won't be able to go inside them.*

🚌 *Zoo bus stop or the Baltic railway sta-tion and then the museum bus stop.*

Kumu Kunsti-muuseum

The Kumu Kunsti-muuseum (Kumu Art Museum) is the main building of the Estonian Art Museum. Its permanent exhibi-tion focuses on the work of Estonian artists from the early 18th century through to the country's 1991 independence. Many of the paintings on display shed light on the attitudes of the time, with works completed during the Soviet occupation of Estonia revealing the uneasy relationship between oppressor and the oppressed.
✉ *Weizenbergi 34/Valge 1,* ☎ *602 6000,* 🖥 *www.ekm.ee* ⏱ *11:00–18:00 Tue–Sun, closed Mon (May–Sep); 11:00–18:00 Wed–Sun, closed Mon & Tue (Oct–Apr).* 🚊 *Kadriorg tram stop or Kumu bus stop.*

Kristjan Raud Majamuuseum

The fifth branch of the Estonian Art Museum, the Kristjan Raud majamuuseum (Kristjan Raud House Museum), highlights the life and work of one of Estonia's most famous artists. Here you can see the rooms where he lived, the studio where he worked and many of his sketches and charcoal drawings.

✉ *Kristjan Raua 8,*
☎ *670 0023,*
🖥 *www.ekm.ee*
🕐 *10:00–17:00 Thu–Sat, closed Sun–Wed.*
♿ *Free admission.*
🚌 *Bus or train to Nõmme.*

Fotomuuseum

Tallinn's 14th-century prison has an altogether different function today and houses the compact Fotomuuseum (Museum of Estonian

Photography). The eclectic collection gives visitors the chance to see a pictorial history of Estonia from 1840–1940. Various old cameras and developing equipment are also on display. Look out for the tiny Minox, invented in Tallinn in the 1930s, which then went on to be manufactured in Rīga.

✉ *Raekoja 4/6,* ☎ *644 8767,* 🖥 *www.linna muuseum.ee*
🕐 *10:30–18:00 Thu–Tue, closed Wed (Mar–Oct); 10:30–17:00 Thu–Tue, closed Wed (Nov–Feb).*
💰 *Free admission on the last Friday of the month.*

Parks and Gardens
Tallinna Botaanikaaed

Situated 10km (6 miles) east of the city centre and home to more than 8000 species of plant, the Tallinna Botaanikaaed (Tallinn Botanical

Gardens) is one of the Estonian capital's best-kept secrets. Strolling through the grounds you are greeted by graceful trees, fragrant roses, shrubs and rock gardens, as well as a variety of perennial plants, lilies, irises and elegant snowdrops. Inside the Glasshouses and Palm House, meanwhile, a diverse range of tropical and subtropical plants thrive. Various seasonal exhibitions that look at everything from houseplants to wild mushrooms complement the permanent collection. One-hour guided tours, conducted in English, Estonian or Russian, can be organized with advance notice.

✉ *Kloostrimetsa 54,* ☎ *606 2666,* 🖥 *www.tba.ee*
🕐 *Outdoor Collection: 11:00–19:00 daily.*
🕐 *Glasshouses and Palm House: 11:00–18:00 daily.*
💰 *Free admission to the outdoor gardens.*

🚌 *Kloostrimetsa bus stop.*

Metsakalmistu

Another Tallinn attraction located out in the Pirita suburb is Metsakalmistu (Forest Cemetery). This burial ground resonates more with Estonian visitors than it does with tourists, as it is the last resting place of several famous Estonians, such as singer Georg Ots, author Anton Hansen Tammsaare, poet Lydia Koidula, the former president Konstantin Päts, composer Rimond Valgre and one-time chess champion Paul Keres. Even if you don't visit the celebrity graves, Metsakalmistu is a tranquil spot.

✉ *Kloostimesta 36,* ☎ *623 9917,* 🖥 *www.kalmistud.ee*
🕐 *09:00–16:00 Mon–Fri, 09:00–14:00 Sat, closed Sun.*
🚌 *Pärnamäe or Metsakalmistu bus stops.*

ACTIVITIES
Sport and Recreation

Tallinn may not be famous in the sporting world, but the Estonian capital still provides plenty of opportunities for getting active, from tennis and swimming to bowling and ice-skating. Alternatively why not go jogging or cycling in the city's parks, lift weights in a public or hotel gym or challenge a companion to a round of golf?

Cycling

While Tallinn's pedestrianized Old Town and busy coastal highway may not be ideal cycling venues, the likes of Kadriorg Park (see page 31) and Pirita Beach (see panel, page 39) are safe environments for even the youngest of cyclists. You can rent bikes or go on a bicycle tour of Tallinn with **City Bike** (✉ Uus 33, ☎ 511 1819, 🖥 www.citybike.ee).

Golf

Some 30km (19 miles) from the Estonian capital, the Tallinn Golf Club Niitvälja, an 18-hole course, has club hire, an on-site restaurant, pro golf shop, sauna and dressing room. If your stay in Tallinn is going to be long, you can even buy a season ticket. **Tallinn Golf Club Niitvälja**, ☎ 678 0454, 🖥 www.egk-golf.ee ⊕ Apr–Oct.

Swimming

Hotel pools are a rarity in Tallinn. If you enjoy a daily dip, check out the **Reval Hotel Olümpia** (🖥 www.revalhotels.com) or the **Tallink Spa & Conference Hotel** (🖥 www.tallinkhotelsgroup.com). On the outskirts of the city the **Pirita Top**

Ice-skating
If you want to join the Estonians in one of their favourite pastimes, Tallinn has two big ice rinks: the Jeti Ice Hall and the Premia Ice Hall. In the winter months an alfresco ice-skating arena comes to Harju Street, just outside St Nicholas's Church (see pages 22–23), in the form of the Uisuplats (the Skating Place).
Jeti Ice Hall, ✉ Suur-Sõjamäe 14b, ☎ 610 1035, 🖥 www.jeti.ee
Premia Ice Hall, ✉ Haabersti 3, ☎ 660 0500, 🖥 www.icearena.ee
Uisuplats, ✉ Harju, ☎ 610 1035, 🖥 www.uisuplats.ee

Below: *Cycling is a very popular pastime in Tallinn and also in the surrounding countryside.*

Spa (🖥 www.topspa.ee) and the **Viimsi Tervis SPA Hotel** (🖥 www.viimsitervis.ee) also have pools. The **Kalev Spa Hotel and Water Park** (🖥 www.kalevspa.ee) has a big pool and a few water slides. There are also municipal pools in **Nõmme** and on **Ehitajate tee**.

Tennis

Estonia has enjoyed moderate success on the world tennis stage, with Kaia Kanepi currently the country's highest-ranked women singles player. At the end of 2007 she was 75th in the WTA rankings. Born in Tallinn on 10 June 1985, she turned profes- sional in 2000 and her highest ranking up to January 2008 was 40th, which she achieved in July 2007; not bad for someone who was just 22 at the time. Anyone inspired by Kanepi can play tennis at the **Falck tennisekeskus** or the **Rocca al Mare Onistar tennisekeskus** (☎ 678 0454).

Bowling

If the weather lets you down, you just want to have fun with the kids or you are plan- ning an alternative night out, then Tallinn has a handful of ten-pin bowling alleys. The large and modern **Ku:lsa:l** and the **Pirita bowlinguklubi** are popular with young and older visitors alike, while **Zelluloosi Bowling** and the **Toolbox** are smaller venues.

Gym

Small fitness centres are more commonly found in Tallinn's hotels than swimming pools; even then they are not a given. For those keen to keep their finely tuned muscles in shape a number of gyms dotted around the capital welcome day visitors.

Spectator Sports
Basketball
Basketball is one of the national sports of Estonia. After the 2007 Eurobasket, the national team came 62nd in the Federation of International Basketball (FIBA) rankings. Tallinn-based teams playing in the main Estonian League (EMKL) include **Tallinna BC Kalev/Crammo**, **BC Pirita**, and **TTÜ korvpalliklubi** (Tallinn Technical University Basketball Club).

Ice Hockey
Ice Hockey is big business in Estonia. In spring 2008 the capital had two teams flying high in the Estonian League: **Tallinn Stars** (🖥 www.hkstars.ee) were second and **Tallinna Purikad** (🖥 www.purikad.ee) were fourth. Estonia also has a successful national team and an under-20s team. For more information visit the website of the **Eesti jäähoki liit** (Estonian Ice Hockey Federation, 🖥 www.esthockey.ee).

Football
The number of football fans in Estonia has been growing steadily since the country became independent in 1991, and it's a hot contender to become the nation's most popular sport. The national stadium, **A Le Coq Arena** (named after a domestic beer), is located in Tallinn; FC Flora are also based here. The **Eesti jalgpalli liit** (Estonian Football Association) is the game's governing body. Tallinn clubs topped the Meistriliiga football league table in 2007. **Tallinna FC Levadia** came first, **Tallinna FC Flora** second, **Tallinn FC TVMK** third and **JK Tallinna Kalev** sixth.

Basketball Lowdown
Tallinna BC Kalev/Crammo, ✉ Sakku Suurhall, Paldiski mnt 104b, ☎ 660 0313, 🖥 www.bckalev.ee
BC Pirita, 🖥 www.bcpirita.ee
TTÜ Korvpalliklubi, ✉ Ehitajate tee 4, ☎ 620 2757, 🖥 www.ttukorvpalliklubi.ee
Baltic Basketball League, 🖥 www.bbl.net
If you want to attend a game ask the tourist office or your hotel concierge to help you, as the websites are largely in Estonian.

Football League
Tallinna FC Levadia, ✉ Vana-Narva 24a, Maardu 74114, ☎ 686 7955, 🖥 www.fclevadia.ee (the team play at the **Kadrioru Staadion**, ✉ Roheline 24, ☎ 601 3510).
Tallinna FC Flora, ✉ A Le Coq Arena, Asula 4c, ☎ 627 9940, 🖥 www.fcflora.ee
Tallinna FC TVMK, ✉ Pärnu mnt 69b, ☎ 626 1502, 🖥 www.fctvmk.ee
JK Tallinna Kalev, ✉ Pärnu mnt 41, ☎ 644 0744, 🖥 www.jkkalev.ee
Eesti Jalgpalli Liit, ✉ A Le Coq Arena, Asula 4c, ☎ 627 9960, 🖥 http://jalgpall.struktuur.ee

ACTIVITIES

<u>**Gay Bars and Clubs**</u>
X-Baar
✉ Sauna 1
☎ 620 9266
Angel Café and Gay Club
✉ Sauna 1
☎ 641 6880
🖳 www.clubangel.ee
Ring Club
✉ Juhkentali 11
☎ 660 5490
🖳 www.ringclub.ee

<u>**Adrenaline Sports**</u>
Tallinn Out There
Rīga office:
✉ Hospitalu 8–49,
Rīga, LV-1013, Latvia
☎ +371 6735 0227
UK office:
☎ +44 208 123 2077
🖳 www.tallinnout
there.com

Alternative Tallinn
Gay and Lesbian Tallinn
While attitudes to homosexuality in Tallinn are more relaxed than in fellow Baltic capitals Rīga and Vilnius, they could hardly be described as enlightened. The city's small gay and lesbian community is gradually becoming more vocal, yet many homosexuals currently choose to stay in the closet.

Tallinn's oldest gay bar, **X-Baar**, is the best place to find out about the local gay scene, while **Angel** is a happening gay nightclub catering mainly to men. Women and non-gay clubbers are admitted at the discretion of the doormen, but it can be tough to get in. Apart from Friday night, which is 'Bisexual Night', the **Ring Club** is exclusively for men.

Adrenaline Sports
Alternative activities tend to be more of the adrenaline kind, with the city and its environs offering opportunities for everything from shooting (both clay pigeon shooting and firing AK-47s and other guns in firing ranges) and canoeing to go-karting and quad biking. **Tallinn Out There** organizes this type of activity, with offices in Rīga and London.

Right: *Angel is a gay nighclub catering mainly for men.*

Fun for Children

Tallinn has a range of family attractions, from ten-pin bowling alleys (*see* page 41) and the FK keskus recreation centre (*see* below) and swimming pools to the city zoo, Pirita beach, a puppet theatre (*see* panel, page 71) and the tourist train that chugs along the Old Town streets. A number of the city's museums are reasonably child friendly, including the Energia keskus (Energy Centre) and the Lastemuuseum (Children's Museum). At the Estonian Open-air Museum (*see* pages 37–38) and Kadriorg Park (*see* page 31) kids also have the space to run around.

Not strictly for kids, **FK keskus** (the FK Centre, ✉ Paldiski mnt 229a, ☎ 687 010, 🖥 www.fkkeskus.ee) also gives adults the chance to get in touch with their inner child with a round on the go-kart track or a game of paintball. There is even a sauna on hand to ease weary limbs. Children have their own go-kart circuit or can stalk one another in a laser quest game.

When compared to big city zoos, like London Zoo, the animal collection at **Loomaaed** (Tallinn Zoo) is modest. The zoo's most celebrated species include sheep, mountain goats, vultures, owls, eagles and cranes. Elephants, tigers, polar bears and crocodiles are just some of the bigger animals that can be found at the zoo.

If you are visiting Tallinn during the summer and the kids fancy spending a day building sandcastles or splashing around in the Baltic Sea, then **Pirita** has a 3km (2-mile) stretch of white sand beach. The beach is also backed by forested parkland, which comes complete with walking and cycling

---

Tallinn Zoo
✉ Paldiski 145/
Ehitajate 150
☎ 694 3300
📱 +372 657 8990
✉ zoo@tallinnlv.ee
🖥 www.tallinnzoo.ee
🕘 09:00–17:00 daily
(Nov–Feb); 09:00–
19:00 daily (Mar–Apr &
Sep–Oct); 09:00–21:00
daily (May–Aug). The
ticket office closes two
hours earlier. The
Ehitajate tee entrance is
closed from Oct–Apr.

European Capital of Culture 2011
Ever since Glasgow held the title of European Capital of Culture in 1990, the accolade, seen as a way of significantly boosting tourism, has become coveted amongst European cities. In 2011 the privilege will fall to Tallinn alongside Turku in Finland. There is every reason to believe that the year will be a resounding success for Tallinn, as well as turning the attention of tourism to Estonia and the rest of the Baltic region.

ACTIVITIES

Freedom Monument

Estonia commemorated the 90th anniversary of its War of Independence on 28 November 2008, and plans are afoot to erect a new Freedom Monument on Harjumägi Hill in Tallinn in the form of a 28m (92ft) high cross-topped column. The motivation for the new statue is to give the capital a symbol of freedom and liberty to match the Freedom Monument in the Latvian capital, Rīga. Similar plans have been shelved in the past due to public opposition, so the completion of the monument is by no means guaranteed.

Old Town Walk

Location: Map A–C3
Distance: about 2.2km (1.4 miles)
Duration: allow 2–3 hours for this walk
Start: Raekoja plats
Finish: Raekoja plats
Route: Heading to the south from Raekoja plats the five sections of the route are Raekoja plats, followed by Niguliste kirik, Komandandi, Toompea and finally returning to Raekoja plats via Pikk jalg and Pikk.

paths, a children's playground and even a mini-golf course.

Energia Keskus

Tallinn's Energia keskus (Energy Centre), otherwise known as the **Tallinn Science and Technology Centre**, is very much a hands-on museum that aims to teach children all about physics in a fun way. Help your young ones understand the laws of gravity as they play with a sand tray, or locate Estonia on an oversized globe. It is popular with school groups during the week. ✉ Põhja 29, ☎ 715 2650, ⌨ www.energia keskus.ee ⏲ 10:00–17:00 Mon–Sat.

Lastemuuseum

Located in the Kalamaja suburb, the Laste-muuseum (Children's Museum, ✉ Kotzebue 16, ☎ 641 3491, ⌨ www.linnamuuseum.ee/lastemuuseum, ⏲ Wed–Sun 10:30–18:00, closed Mon & Tue) looks at the evolution of games and toys from the Middle Ages to the present. Toy cars, model planes, dolls and dolls' houses are just some of the highlights. Younger children might appreciate the chance to play with Lego bricks, make their own toys or watch cartoons.

Walking Tour
Old Town Walk

A walk that takes in many of the Old City's key sights starts at **Raekoja plats** (Town Hall Square). After snapping the iconic **Tallinna raekoda** (Tallinn Town Hall, *see* page 15) and visiting one of Europe's oldest pharmacies, **Raeapteek** (*see* page 16), head south down Kullassepa and turn right onto Niguliste where you will find the medieval **Niguliste**

kirik (St Nicholas's Church, *see* pages 22–23).

Retrace your steps to the corner and head south down Harju to the Mayeri steps and up to Komandandi. Here Harjumägi Hill should now be the proud home of Tallinn's new **Freedom Monument** (scheduled to be unveiled by early 2009; *see* panel, page 46). Continue west along Komandandi to **Kiek in de kök** (*see* pages 17–18), where you can gen up on Tallinn's defensive history or visit the **Bastionide Käigud** (Secret Tunnels, *see* page 18) on a pre-arranged tour.

At the junction of Komandandi and Toompea turn right and walk up to **Lossi plats** (Castle Square), where the highlight is the ornate **Aleksander Nevski katedraal** (Alexander Nevsky Cathedral, *see* pages 26–27). **Toompea loss** (Toompea Castle, *see* page 25), **Pikk Hermann** (Tall Hermann's Tower, *see* page 25) and the **Riigikogu** (Parliament, *see* page 26) are also located on Castle Square.

Now make your way to the **Patkuli Viewing Platform** by heading north along Toom-Kooli, and then Rahukohtu via Kirku plats and the **Toom-kirk** (Dome Church, *see* pages 27–28). The Kohtuotsa Viewing Platform is northeast of Kirku plats.

You can return to the Lower Town via

Self-guided Tours

If you want to learn more about Tallinn's sights, but at your own pace, you can hire four- and six-hour audio guides from:

Audio Guide Ltd
✉ Akadeemia 19
☎ 655 6633
🖥 www.audioguide.ee
iPod audio can also be rented from the tourist information office and some hotels. A downloadable version should soon be available on
🖥 www.euroguide.com

Below: *Town Hall Square, start of the Old Town Walking Tour, is also a great place for outdoor refreshments.*

Alexander Nevsky Cathedral and the pedestrianized street that travels east/northeast to Pikk jalg. Pikk jalg then becomes Pikk, from here Voorimeha will take you back to Raekoja plats.

Organized Tours

Various organized tours are available in and around Tallinn, from hop-on and hop-off bus tours and combined bus and walking city tours to specialized itineraries (see Alternative Tallinn, page 44). It is also possible to book tailor-made trips for groups.

Bus Tours

Tallinn City Tour hop-on and hop-off bus tours run on three different routes. The **Red Line** concentrates on the town centre and starts outside the Sokos Hotel Viru on Viru väljak, just east of the Viru Gates. Subsequent stops include Toompea, the Radisson SAS, the Park Hotel, Kumu Art Museum and Kadriorg Palace. This circular route returns passengers to Viru.

The **Green Line** also starts and finishes at the Sokos Hotel Viru before whisking passengers off to Pirita via Kadriorg Palace and the Maarjamäe War Memorial. For those wanting to visit the Estonian Open-air Museum (see pages 37–38) and Tallinn Zoo (see page 45), taking the **Blue Line** to the suburb of Rocca al Mare is a good idea.

Bus and Walking Tours

Travel to Baltics operate a combined bus and walking tour of Tallinn, which lasts for two and a half hours. Pick-up is from major hotels and the port. The coach takes in key sights like Kadriorg Palace and Pirita, while

---

Spa Therapy

If pampering is integral to your idea of a good holiday, then help is at hand in Tallinn's spas:
Day Spa, ✉ Vana-Posti 4, ☎ 641 8701, 🖥 www.dayspa.ee
Reval Day Spa, ✉ Pikk 7, ☎ 642 2047, 🖥 www.revaldayspa.eu
Babor Spa, ✉ Narva mnt 5, ☎ 664 0488, 🖥 www.baborspa.ee
City Spa, ✉ Rävala pst 4, ☎ 640 0200, 🖥 www.cityspa.ee
Shnelli Day Spa & Salon, ✉ Toompuiestee 37, ☎ 631 0160, 🖥 www.spalife.ee
Kalev Spa, ✉ Aia 18, ☎ 6493 350, 🖥 www.kalevspa.ee
Spalife, ✉ Roosikrantsi 11, ☎ 667 6227, 🖥 www.spalife.ee (for men)
Aqua Spa, ✉ Tallink Spa & Conference Hotel, Sadama 11, ☎ 630 1028, 🖥 www.tallinkhotelsgroup.com
Medi Spa, ✉ Pirita Top Spa Hotell, Regati pst 1, ☎ 639 8718, 🖥 www.topspa.ee

---

the walking component lets you explore the pedestrianized Old City. Tours are given in English, Swedish, German and Finnish. **Tallinn Out There** also organize a combined bus and walking tour, which lasts three hours.

Bicycle Tours

City Bike offer visitors the chance to explore Tallinn on a bicycle, or on a tour that approximates a fitness walk with poles and is called the Nordic Walking Tour. The two-wheeled tour takes two hours and covers 14km (9 miles), taking cyclists out to Kadriorg Place and Pirita. The 3–4km (2–2.5-mile) walking tour meanwhile concentrates on the Old Town.

Excursions

If you have more than a few days in Tallinn and want to see more of Estonia, **Tallinn Out There** organize day trips to Lahemaa National Park (*see* pages 80–81) and the Estonian Open-air Museum (*see* pages 37–38). Excursions also take in destinations like Pärnu (*see* page 82) and Haapsalu (*see* page 81). To cycle around Laheema National Park, book a tour with **City Bike**.

Above: *The Nordic Walking Tour, which concentrates on the Old Town, is a good way of seeing the sights in Tallinn.*

Tour Operators

Tallinn City Tour, ✉ Kadaka 62a, ☎ 627 9080, 💻 www.citytour.ee

Travel to Baltics, ☎ 610 8616, 💻 www. travel2baltics.com

City Bike, ✉ Uus 33, ☎ 511 1819, 💻 www. citybike.ee

Tallinn Out There, *see* panel, page 44.

Above: *Tallinn is a good place to find amber jewellery.*

Amber

Valued for its rich orangey-brown colour, amber is widely used in jewellery and other ornamental items. Contrary to popular belief it is not a mineral and therefore not a precious or even semi-precious stone. Instead it is the result of the fossilization of tree sap or resin. The most expensive pieces of amber are generally at least 30 million years old, with the semi- or subfossilized resin more accurately called copal. Cheap imitations are also widely available, so beware.

SHOPPING

Tallinn boasts a surprisingly diverse shopping experience, from Old Town boutiques, which sell everything from cheap and tacky tourist memorabilia to exclusive handmade jewellery, to modern shopping centres and colourful markets.

Shopping Streets

Vanalinn is awash with small shops selling everything from elegant amber jewellery and unique paintings to the kind of mass-produced keepsakes that you find in

any tourist city. A handful of small art galleries are located on Pikk jalg and Lühike jalg, while the streets that branch away from Raejoka plats (Town Hall Square) boast a cluster of souvenir shops selling a range of handicrafts like ceramics, hand knits, linen and wooden toys. If you fancy a rummage through other people's relics then there are a couple of antique/junk shops on Pikk. This list is by no means exhaustive and half the fun of shopping in the Old Town is just wandering around popping into any store that catches your eye.

Shopping Centres
Foorum

This chic mall is the place to come to buy high-end brand goods like Calvin Klein clothes, Timber and Camper shoes and Tommy Hilfiger designer clothing. Home to the Babor Spa (*see* panel, page 48), the trendy Argentinean restaurant Buenos Aries and St Patrick's Pub – you can easily spend a whole day and night at Foorum.

✉ *Narva mnt 5,* 🖳 *www.foorum shopping.ee* 🕓 *09:00–21:00 daily.*

Tallinna Kaubamaja

A Tallinn institution dating to the 1960s, this large department store still manages to keep up with its rivals. Retail addicts will be in shopping heaven, with everything from clothing and home wares to an up-market food hall located under one roof.

✉ *Gonsiori 2,* ☎ *667 3100,* 🖳 *www. kaubamaja.ee* 🕓 *09:00–21:00 Mon–Sat, 10:00–19:00 Sun.*

Viru Keskus

The new Viru shopping centre is actually linked to Tallinna kaubamaja (*see* above) by a glass walkway. Here you

will find a variety of stores, restaurants, cafés, bars and the Sokos Hotel Viru. A number of Estonia's most prominent fashion designers also have outlets in the centre, or outside on Viru väljak.

✉ *Viru väljak 4/6,* ☎ *610 1400,* 🖳 *www. virukeskus.com* 🕓 *09:00–21:00 daily.*

Shops
Estonian Handicraft House

This souvenir shop is in a different class to many of the others and sells high-quality handicrafts from around Estonia. If you are looking for a special piece of jewellery, delicate ceramics or warm (hand-knitted) winter woollies then this could be the place for you. There is also a Folk Art Gallery on site where you can visit various workshops.

✉ *Pikk 22,* ☎ *660 4772,* 🖳 *www. folkart.ee* 🕓 *09:00–18:00 Mon–Sat, closed Sun.*

Best Buys
• **Vana Tallinn**
A potent rum-flavoured alcoholic drink.
• **Amber souvenirs**
Choose from cheap and cheerful goods from the market stall or designer pieces in expensive jewellers.
• **Woollens**
Bag a pair of hand-knitted gloves, scarf, hat or jumper to keep you warm in winter.
• **Ceramics**
Take a piece of Tallinn home with you in the form of a replica Town Hall, merchant house or church.
• **Honey**
Get a sweet local variety in a mini-market.
• **Handicrafts**
Hand-woven linen and wooden toys or utensils are other quintessential Tallinn souvenirs.
• **Kalev chocolates**
These tasty treats will go down well at home.

Shopping

Tax-free Shopping

Non-European Union residents can claim a partial refund of Estonian value added tax/sales tax. Where the VAT is 18% (currently the standard rate in Estonia) you will get back around 12% after handling expenses, but where a lower rate of 5% VAT has been charged this is not refundable. Only purchases over 2500EEK made in a single shop in one day qualify. Shops displaying the tax-free shopping signs participate in the scheme and you must ask the assistant for a tax-free shopping cheque at the point of sale. This should be stamped by customs when you leave the EU. For more information visit 🖳 www.global refund.com

Aurum

If you are yearning after a classy memento of your visit to Tallinn, then a piece of bespoke jewellery could be the ticket. This Old Town jeweller sells necklaces, earrings, bracelets and rings in a range of modern and classical styles, alongside silverware, watches, pearls and pens.
✉ *Kullassepa 4,* ☎ *644 9874,* 🖳 *www. aurum.ee* ⊕ *11:00– 19:00 Mon–Fri, 10:00– 15:00 Sat, closed Sun.*

Hula

Make a statement and purchase a truly unique piece of clothing. Everything sold by Hula is the work of the fashion students studying at the Estonian Academy of Arts. If the designer makes the big time the garment that you buy might be worth a fortune one day.
✉ *Pikk 41,* ☎ *646 4369,* 🖳 *www.hula.ee* ⊕ *Irregular opening hours.*

Reval Antik

This Old Town antique shop is a real gem. Among the many items on sale you will find the likes of Art Deco furniture, gilt-edged mirrors, ornate silver sugar bowls, ceramics, metal ware, 20th-century dolls and even Russian icons. If you are hunting for cheap knick-knacks, this isn't the place for you.
✉ *Harju 13,* ☎ *644 0747,* 🖳 *www.reval-antique.ee* ⊕ *10:00–18:00 Mon– Fri, 10:00–17:00 Sat, closed Sun.*

Markets
Knit Market

Tallinn's older residents have been selling hand-knitted jumpers, gloves and hats, etc., at the 'sweater wall' for several decades. Goods on sale here tend to be of decent quality and are reasonably priced.
✉ *Corner of Viru and Müürivahe,* ⊕ *09:00– 17:00 daily.*

MARKETS

Mere Art Market

This is another good source of hand-knitted clothing.
✉ Mere pst 1,
🕐 09:00–17:00 daily.

Merekeskus

Goods on sale here are shady to say the least, with pirated CDs and fake brand names all part of the mix. The frequent police raids, however, don't appear to deter the counterfeiters.
✉ Mere pst 10,
🕐 09:00–19:00 daily.

Kadaka Turg

The sprawling Kadaka Market sells everything from cheap imitation jewellery to Soviet memorabilia. Many locals dismiss it as a junkyard and they may have a point.
✉ Corner of Tammsaare and Mustamäe tee,
🕐 09:00–19:00 daily.

Bõrsi Käik Art Market

This colourful art market comes to an alley between Pikk and Lai streets during the main tourist season.
✉ Pikk 17,
🕐 09:00–19:00 daily (summer).

Keskturg

Generally the preserve of locals, Keskturg (Central Market) sells fresh food as well as bargain clothes.
✉ Keldrimäe 9,
🕐 08:00–18:00 daily.

Balti Jaama Turg

This local market at the railway station sells a mishmash of items, from spare car parts to raw meat. It is not very salubrious and is best avoided after dark.
✉ Kopli 1,
🕐 08:00–19:00 Mon–Sat, 08:00–17:00.

Above: *Modern wool craft makes a good souvenir.*

At the Market

Whether you are shopping at the tourist-orientated markets in Tallinn's Old Town or at one of the city's local markets, don't be afraid to bargain, even if some of the sellers do look a bit fearsome. If you are buying more than one item you are more likely to get a discount. The old walking away trick can pay dividends. It is also a good idea to keep an eye on your valuables, as crowded marketplaces are popular with pick-pockets.

ACCOMMODATION

Above: *The Radisson SAS is great for business travellers.*

Room with a View

Rooms with views used to be in short supply in Tallinn, but that has all changed. In the 1990s it was the tower hotels outside the Old Town, in the form of the Radisson SAS (see page 57) and the Olümpia (see page 57), that offered the only views. On opening in 2007 the Swissotel (see page 58) offered a whole new range of views, unsurprising as it resides in the highest building in town so you can choose from a multitude of expansive vistas. The aforementioned are all luxury hotels, but there are some cheaper options that offer more affordable views in the shape of City Hotel Portus (see page 58) and Go Hotel Shnelli (see page 58).

WHERE TO STAY

In line with other European capitals, hotels in Tallinn are graded according to a star system, with five stars the highest rating and one star the lowest. Standards, though, vary and you would be unwise to make a reservation based solely on the number of stars that a property has been awarded. When it comes to hotel accommodation visitors also have the choice between boutique Old Town properties and larger business hotels. At the cheaper end of the scale there are also backpacker hostels, guesthouses and rooms in private homes. For those on a tight budget, try Tallinn City Camping (⊠ Pirita 28, Tallinn 10127, ☎ 613 7322, 🖥 www.tallinn-city-camping.ee) ◐ mid-May to mid-Sep.

Regardless of your budget it is wise to plan in advance. Big events and the sheer volume of tourists who descend upon Tallinn in the height of summer means that rooms in the Old Town in particular are often fully booked. Late booking frequently means that you will pay higher prices then too. No matter what the season if you arrive in Tallinn without a reservation you may have to stay further away from the city centre than you had originally planned.

Another option that can be surprisingly affordable is to rent an apartment. A variety of agents arrange short (as little as one night) or longer stays in Tallinn. Old Town locations are very popular and tend to be in short supply, but there is also a wealth of accommodation available on the fringes of the Old City.

Old Town

• *LUXURY*

Schlossle (Map A–C3)
When it comes to both location and old-world luxury the boutique Schlossle is hard to beat, which is why it is often the bolthole of choice for visiting celebrities and royalty including Prince Charles. Tallinn's oldest five-star hotel has long been impressing guests with its attentive service, first-class location and grandeur. It is perhaps the best hotel in the country. ✉ *Pühavaimu 13/15, Tallinn 10123,* ☎ *699 7700,* 📠 *699 7777,* 💻 *www.schlossle-hotels.com*

St Petersbourg

(Map A–B3)
More affordable than its illustrious sibling, the Schlossle, this central hotel offers luxurious rooms. It can, though, be a bit noisy at times with noise from the street and, in one instance, the sauna located immediately above the room.

✉ *Rataskaevu 7, Tallinn 10123,* ☎ *628 6500,* 📠 *628 6565,* 💻 *www.schlossle-hotels.com*

Three Sisters

(Map A–D1)
Check into this five-star design hotel and find yourself a part of Tallinn's history, literally, and very much part of its modern map too. Located within the 16th-century walls, the hotel also boasts a fine-dining restaurant and a wine bar.
✉ *Pikk 71/Trolli 2, Tallinn 10133,* ☎ *630 6300,* 📠 *630 6301,* 💻 *www.threesisters hotel.com*

Barons (Map A–C4)

This luxurious Old Town boutique hotel is a favourite with business and leisure visitors alike. Traditional period features combine seamlessly with high-speed Internet and satellite TVs.
✉ *Suur-Karja 7, Tallinn 10140,* ☎ *699 9700,* 📠 *699 9710,* 💻 *www. baronshotel.ee*

Domina Inn City

(Map A–C4)
Great if you want to relax in comfort in the Old Town. Service is smooth here and it is worth paying extra for one of the 'superior' rooms, which tend to be bigger, with some boasting views too.
✉ *Vana-Posti 11/13, Tallinn 10146,* ☎ *681 3900,* 📠 *681 3901,* 💻 *www.domina hotels.com*

Savoy (Map A–C4)

Housed in a lovely 19th-century building, this old dame was brought back to life in 2006 and now boasts just 43 individual rooms. The style is understated and pleasantly refined.
✉ *Suur-Karja 17/19, Tallinn 10148,* ☎ *680 6688,* 📠 *680 6689,* 💻 *www.savoyhotel.ee*

Telegraaf (Map A–C3)

One of the newest hotels in the Old Town is also one of the best. Housed in a gorgeous building that used to be a bank, this is a

lovely place to stay –
go for the historic part
of the hotel, not the
newer annex.
✉ Vene 9, Tallinn
10123, ☎ 600 0600,
🖷 600 0601, 🖳 www.
telegraafhotel.com

Viru Inn (Map A–C3)
Not to be confused
with the hulking
tower hotel of the
same name, this little
hideaway sits on one
of the prettiest and
busiest streets in the
Old Town. You can
recline in this 15th-
century retreat bathed
in layers of history;
you can also enjoy a
free morning sauna.
Complimentary airport
pick-ups too.
✉ Viru 8, Tallinn
10140, ☎ 611 7600,
🖷 641 8367, 🖳 www.
viruinn.ee

• *MID-RANGE*
**Merchant's House
Hotel** (Map A–C3)
Straddling two 14th-
and 16th-century
properties, this hotel
impresses guests with
neat original touches
like wooden beams

and restored fireplaces.
Rooms are modern
and comfortable and a
range of massages
(including a decadent
chocolate option) are
also on offer.
✉ Dunkri 4/6, Tallinn
10123, ☎ 697 7500,
🖷 697 7501, 🖳 www.
merchantshouse
hotel.com

**Baltic Hotel
Imperial** (Map A–B2)
Situated at the foot of
Toompea Hill the
Imperial, with its 32
contemporary rooms
and suites, sauna, hot
tub and free Internet
access, is another
good bet, as well as
being decent value.
✉ Nunne 14, Tallinn
10133, ☎ 627 4800,
🖷 627 4801, 🖳 www.
imperial.ee

**Romeo Family
Hotel** (Map A–C4)
This friendly family-
run bolthole offers
some of the best value
accommodation in the
Old Town. Choose
from their trio of
doubles or book one
of their eight apart-

ments for a bit more
space. You can drift
back through the
centuries without
damaging your bank
balance too much.
✉ Suur-Karja 18,
Tallinn, ☎ 644 4255,
🖷 660 9588, 🖳 www.
romeofamily.ee

• *BUDGET*
Braavo (Map A–D2)
This two-star was a
welcome addition to
the local budget hotel
scene when it opened
in 2007. Great value
accommodation
options include
singles, doubles and
family apartments with
their own kitchenettes.
Free wireless Internet
throughout.
✉ Aia 20, Tallinn
10111, ☎ 699 9777,
🖷 699 9770, 🖳 www.
braavo.ee

Meriton Old Town
(Map A–C1)
Located near Tallinn
Port, this reasonably
characterful hotel
boasts 41 *en-suite*
rooms. Great Internet
rates are often avail-
able here.

✉ *Lai 49, Tallinn 10149,* ☎ *614 1 300,* ✆ *614 1311,* 🖥 *www. meritonhotels.com*

Tallinn Backpackers

(Map A–D2)
Bag a bed in one of the 16-, 10- or six-bed dorms (the bigger the dorm, the cheaper the price) at this friendly central hostel. They also have singles, doubles and triples available on nearby Viru.
✉ *Olevimägi 11, Tallinn 10123,* ☎ *644 0298,* 🖥 *www.tallinn backpackers.com*

Old House

(Map A–D2)
Providing accommo-dation in dormitories, single, twin and quad rooms at its guest-house and hostel, as well as private accom-modation, the Old House should have something to suit your wallet. It is by no means glamorous but offers decent value.
✉ *Uus 22, 10111,* ☎ *641 1464,* ✆ *641 1604,* 🖥 *www.oldhouse.ee*

Outside the Old Town

• *LUXURY*
Euroopa (Map B–D2)
This four-star hotel is in a location both handy for the nearby port and also for walking into the Old Town. Geared towards both the business and tourist markets, it boasts half a dozen meetings rooms, as well as a fitness room and sauna, which guests can use free of charge. Book a 'Business Room' for a balcony where you can watch the hulking ferries lumber in and out of the increasingly busy port.
✉ *Paadi 5, Tallinn 10151,* ☎ *669 9777,* ✆ *669 9770,* 🖥 *www. euroopa.ee*

Radisson SAS

(Map B–D4)
No fewer than 15 con-ference rooms make this bright modern hotel on the edge of the Old Town perfect for business travellers; and the rooms are some of the largest in the city. In addition, great Old Town views are to be had from the upper levels.
✉ *Ravala 3, Tallinn 10143,* ☎ *682 3000,* ✆ *682 3001,* 🖥 *www. radissonsas.com*

Domina Inn Ilmarine

(Map B–C1)
This is one of the new breed of hotel down at the rapidly trans-forming port area and is handy if you are catching an early ferry to or from Helsinki and still want a very comfortable place to bed down for the night.
✉ *Pohja 23,* ☎ *614 0900,* ✆ *614 0901,* 🖥 *www.domina hotels.com*

Reval Hotel Olümpia

(Map B–D5)
One of the older lux-ury hotels in the city which was the place to stay in the years after independence. A real monster with 390 rooms, a conference centre and a swim-ming pool. Still up there with comfy

rooms and a nod to the business crowd, with free wireless Internet throughout. ⊠ Liivalaia 33, Tallinn 10118, ☎ 631 5333, ⌶ 631 5325, 🖳 www. revalhotels.com

Swissotel

(Map B–D4)
A room with a view is not hard to find in this new tower hotel situated in the Estonian capital's tallest building. As well as 238 rooms, the hotel boasts a spa, full conference and incentive facilities, a swimming pool and a modern gym.
⊠ Tornimae 3, Tallinn 10145, ☎ 624 0000, ⌶ 624 0001, 🖳 www. swissotel.com

• MID-RANGE
City Hotel Portus

(Map B–E2)
A combination of reasonable prices and a great location make the Portus hard to beat. The rooms are not elaborate, but many have good views and all come

with air-conditioning, satellite TV and Wi-fi. ⊠ Uus-Sadama 23, Tallinn 10120, ☎ 680 6600, ⌶ 680 6601, 🖳 www.portus.ee

Go Hotel Shnelli

(Map B–B1)
Train buffs will love this hotel as it is part of the city's main railway station. It is also right on the edge of the Old Town so non-trainspotters will be happy here too. Good views of Toompea from some of the rooms are another plus. The Shnelli Day Spa is also located here.
⊠ Toompuiestee 37, Tallinn 10133, ☎ 631 0100, ⌶ 631 0101, 🖳 www.gohotels.ee

Reval Inn

(Map B–D1)
Providing comparatively basic but comfortable and affordable accommodation just five minutes' walk from the Old Town, the 163-room Reval Inn also has a café, complimentary

Internet terminals and Wi-Fi access.
⊠ Sadama 1, Tallinn 10111, ☎ 667 8700, ⌶ 667 8800, 🖳 www. revalinn.com

Tatari 53 Hotell

(Map B–B6)
Unfussy 36-room hotel that offers cheap and surprisingly cheerful accommodation. There is a choice of twin and double rooms, and breakfast is served in the room that doubles up as a rudimentary restaurant. Look out for 10% discounts on Internet bookings.
⊠ Tatari 53, Tallinn 10134, ☎ 640 5150, ⌶ 640 5151, 🖳 www. tatari53.ee

• BUDGET
Hotel G9 (Map B–D4)
This small and cosy option is within easy walking distance of the Old Town. With only 23 double rooms, booking ahead is essential as this is one of the best bargains in town. One downside is that they don't

serve breakfast, though there are plenty of good café and restaurant options nearby.

✉ *Gonsiori 9, Tallinn 10117,* ☎ *626 7100,* ✆ *626 7102,* 🖳 *www. hotelg9.ee*

Further Afield

• *MID-RANGE*

Ecoland (Map C–G1)
This unpretentious three-star is located in the forests on the edge of the city and is a relaxed place to stay. Enjoy a mud bath, try some traditional food in their restaurant or rent one of their bungalows for extra privacy; you'll feel like the city is a million miles away.

✉ *Randvere tee 115, Tallinn 19913,* ☎ *605 1999,* ✆ *605 1998,* 🖳 *www.ecoland.ee*

Poska Villa

(Map B–F3)
Poska Villa is a lovely wooden house, dating back to the early 20th century, that is located out by pretty Kadriorg Park. They

have a choice of single and double rooms, with the best the romantic trio of doubles that nestle in the attic.

✉ *Poska 15, Tallinn,* ☎ *601 3601,* ✆ *601 3754,* 🖳 *www. hot.ee/poskavilla*

Hotell Susi

(Map C–E4)
If you can stand the marauding Finnish tour groups that sometimes descend on this three-star it is a decent place to stay. Amenities are good for a mid-range hotel, with a hair salon, business facilities and even a couple of saunas, the largest of which can cater for ten guests. Internet discounts are often available.

✉ *Peterburi tee 48, Tallinn,* ☎ *630 3200,* ✆ *630 3400,* 🖳 *www. susi.ee*

Tähetorni

(Map C–A5)
Quite what you will make of this suburban home-cum-red-brick

pseudo castle is anyone's guess, but Tähetorni is nothing if not unique. It is located almost 10km (6 miles) from the centre, so don't stay here if you enjoy midnight strolls back to your hotel, though rooms are of a decent size and they also have their own restaurant, bar and conference room.

✉ *Tähetorni 16, Tallinn 11625,* ☎ *677 9100,* ✆ *677 9110,* 🖳 *www.thotell.ee*

• *BUDGET*

Dzingel (Map C–C6)
With bed and breakfast for two people costing around 50 euros a night, as well as free on-site parking and complimentary use of the sauna, this hotel is deservedly a popular budget option. The only drawback is its location 6km (4 miles) from the Old Town.

✉ *Männiku tee 89, Tallinn 11213,* ☎ *610 5201,* ✆ *610 5245,* 🖳 *www.dzingel.ee*

Alexi Villa

(Map C–B6)

Nestled out in a quieter area 5km (3 miles) away from the Old Town maelstrom in the Nõmme district. The choice is between five double rooms and one more luxurious suite for four. Free wireless Internet is available to all guests and a sauna and meeting room are on hand too.

✉ *Sihi, Tallinn 11622,* ☎ *670 0096,* ☏ *650 6221,* 🖥 *www.alexi.ee*

Pirita Cloister Guesthouse

(Map C–F2)

One of the most bizarre places to stay in Tallinn is out near the yachting marina at Pirita. The prices are suitably frugal, but rooms are perfectly modern and comfortable. If you want something a little different, a guesthouse run by Swedish nuns may be just the thing for you.

✉ *Merivalja tee 18, Tallinn 11911,* ☎ *605 5000,* ☏ *605 5006,* 🖥 *www.pirita klooster.ee*

Stroomi (Map C–B2)

Tallinn may not exactly be regarded as a beach destination, but you are within easy reach of a beach at this hotel, so you can impress friends at home with your tales of swimming in the Baltic. The raffish area around could at best be described as 'Soviet chic', but the rooms are fine and there is a restaurant, beauty salon and sauna if the weather is not conducive to beach bumming.

✉ *Randla 11, Tallinn 10315,* ☎ *630 4200,* ☏ *630 4500,* 🖥 *www.stroomi.ee*

Apartment Rental

For those who would prefer their stay in the city to be self-catering, or are planning to spend more than a few days in Tallinn and want to minimize their accommodation costs without sacrificing quality, then a rented apartment can be a good idea. There are a number of agencies springing up all over Tallinn, but beware of 'companies' who don't have their own office and make sure you know the exact location so your 'easy walk to the Old Town' does not end up being a bus-changing epic in from the suburbs. The companies listed below are reasonably well established.

Apartment

This is a friendly and easy-to-deal-with apartment rental service who provide an eclectic range of accommodation options from simple, small boltholes through to more expansive luxury hideaways. Some apartments even have access to Jacuzzis and saunas. A plus is that they offer complimentary airport transfers.

✉ *Pilve 4, Tallinn 10122,* ☎ *504 5444,* ✆ *660 5818,* 🖥 *www.apartment.ee*

Erel International

(Map B–D4)

A variety of one-, two- and three-bedroom apartments, many with an Old Town location. They even have one right on Old Town Square, which has to be the best location in town. Airport transfers are available.

✉ *Tartu mnt 14, Tallinn 10117,* ☎ *610 8780,* ✆ *610 8790,* 🖥 *www.erel.ee*

Ites Apartments

(Map A–C4)

This apartment renting company has a choice of one-, two- and three-bedroom flats. Handily decent photos and descriptions of them are available on their website. They have some good Old Town locations available and are amenable to both short- and long-stay rentals.

✉ *Harju 6, Tallinn 10130,* ☎ *631 0637,* 🖥 *www.ites.ee*

Residence Apartments

(Map A–C4)

This classy company specializes in some plush apartments, primarily in Old Town locations. They can arrange one-, two- and four-bedroom options, which are all detailed on their website (this has to be the most treasured website address of any accommodation provider in Estonia). Unusually, breakfast is included in room rates, as are airport transfers.

✉ *Suur-Karja 23, Tallinn 10148,* ☎ *628 2295,* ✆ *628 2296,* 🖥 *www. accommodation.ee*

Bed & Breakfast

The concept of B&B is still somewhat in its infancy in Tallinn, though staying in private houses has a long tradition in itself. Things are slowly starting to change and there is an agency that specializes in this type of accommodation. You get the chance to interact with local families, though sometimes the experience can be vastly different from a traditional British-style Bed & Breakfast, which may not suit everyone – shared bathrooms are common.

Rasastra Bed & Breakfast

(Map A–E3)

This agency has been operating since the 1990s, offering B&B accommodation both in the Old Town and further out, as well as across the rest of the country. It is actually listed under 'Family Accommodation' on their website as opposed to their apartments, which they also rent out.

✉ *Mere pst 4, Tallinn 10111,* ☎ *661 6291,* 🖥 *www.bed breakfast.ee*

Honey

In the past many Estonians made their own honey, and although apiculture tends to be the preserve of specialist farms today, *mesi* (honey) remains a popular food. You just need to pop along to one of the city's supermarkets or the Central Market, where you will find myriad varieties of honey (e.g. light, dark, heather, wild, linden and dandelion), to see this for yourself. Each type has a subtly different flavour depending upon the blossoms that the bees have been allowed to take nectar from. **Estonian Meekook** (layered honey cake) is a popular dessert.

EATING OUT
What to Eat

Estonian food is influenced by the country's temperate climate, its agricultural heritage and centuries of German, Danish, Swedish and Russian rule. During long, cold winters Estonians typically eat hearty meat dishes. Pork is the main meat, with beef and poultry also widely eaten. In summer, meals tend to be lighter.

At one time poorer Estonians would have grown their own grains, potatoes, cabbage, beets, peas and turnips and foraged for wild berries (e.g. strawberries, blueberries and raspberries) and mushrooms. Although most people now buy these, they are still integral to the average diet. *Kartulid* (potatoes) accompany almost every popular traditional dish. Porridge and *Leib* (a sour black rye bread) are also both staples. The tradition of preserving vegetables by pickling them continues, so look out for sauerkraut, pickled mushrooms, pickled pumpkin and dill pickles.

Fish is another fundamental part of the Estonian diet. Historically, people living in the hinterland visited the coast annually to buy preserved (dried, smoked and salted) fish in bulk. Tallinn, though, is a coastal city and its inhabitants have long enjoyed fresh, as well as preserved seafood. The most commonly eaten catches include herring, salmon, perch, flounder and sprat, while crayfish is considered a luxury.

Dairy favourites include cheese, butter, milk, cream, *Kohupiim* (similar to cottage cheese, but a little sweeter) and *kefir* (sour milk). Desserts often incorporate fruit (fresh, dried or stewed), nuts and cream. Semolina and pancakes are both popular puddings, as are berry pies and cakes, *Kohupiim*- or curd-topped biscuits and sweet breads.

Today most Estonians live in urban areas and work long hours. It is no surprise then that both convenience and fast food have become increasingly commonplace in the national diet. Foods from around the world are also available and a new emphasis on healthy living is seeing many people opt for leaner low-fat products. This said, many Estonians still regularly eat a traditional and simple hot meal consisting of meat, cabbage and potatoes. One of the most common starters is soup. Visitors tend to stick to the clear broth varieties, but Russian-style borsht and milky rice soups are also widely available.

Other typical Estonian foods include *Kama* (a specific type of flour), *Kotlet* (best approximated as an onion burger), *Veri-vorst* (blood sausage), *sült* (jellied meat), potato salad spiced up with sausage, sour mayonnaise, egg and dill pickles, cabbage rolls (minced meat wrapped in cabbage leaves) and cabbage stew.

What to Drink

As a result of globalization Estonians essentially drink the same things as people in westernized nations throughout the world. Coffee and teas are staples, for grown-ups

Booze Cruises
Finns have long travelled to Tallinn to stock up on cheap alcohol, much in the same way that Brits might nip over to Calais or Bologne to do the same. Alcohol is not only more expensive in Finland but the sale of hard liquor is also strictly controlled. The Finnish authorities regard high pricing and regulated sales as tools for tackling its many problems related to alcohol abuse. Finns are not the only people arriving in Tallinn with cheap booze in mind, and the Estonian capital is becoming increasingly popular with British stag parties (groups of men enjoying a raucous weekend as they celebrate an impending marriage).

Opposite: *Healthy salads are on the menu in Tallinn's bountiful cafés and restaurants.*

at least, although – unlike the British – Estonians don't usually add milk to their hot drinks. In preference coffee is drunk strong and black with lots of sugar added. Water, fruit juice and carbonated drinks like Coca-Cola are also popular. Companies bottling spring water (both sparkling and still) have enjoyed the same kind of marketing success that they have had in the UK and you can buy bottled water in almost any shop, café or restaurant in Tallinn.

Traditional drinks

If you are after something a bit more traditional, you can try *kvass* (a non-alcoholic yeast drink), fresh berry juice or birch juice (fresh or fermented), as well as the aforementioned *kefir* (sour milk). If this isn't what you had in mind then Estonia also has some long-established alcoholic drinks.

Alcohol

With a high per capita consumption it is fair to say that *õlu* (beer) is one of Estonia's favourite, if not the nation's favourite, tipples. There are five main breweries in Estonia, with Karksi, Pärnu, Saku, Tartu and Viru brewing litres of richly flavoured beer, which can provide a stark contrast to the often mild, weakly flavoured brews churned out by some multinational corporations.

In keeping with global trends the main breweries have diversified their production, with light beer,

Below: *Wine is one of the most popular choices in Estonia when it comes to alcoholic drinks.*

blond beer, malty beer, beer flavoured with lemon, honey and even pomegranate, ice beer, porter (stout), and beers with a high percentage of alcohol (Saku Presidendi, for example, is 10% by volume) served alongside more traditional pilsners and dark beers. An ever more diverse range of alcopops and flavoured ciders are also on offer in Tallinn.

Tallinn's bars and restaurants have as wide a choice of alcoholic drinks as you would find in any modern city, but in terms of spirits, Estonian vodka is the most traditional. Fruit-infused wines and liqueurs are also popular with Estonians.

Vana Tallinn

Definitely an acquired taste, Vana Tallinn is a strong rum-flavoured liqueur, whose key ingredients include cinnamon, citrus oils, vanilla and, you've guessed it, rum. It can be drunk on ice or mixed with beer or coffee; Vana Tallinn is also sneaking in to a number of cocktails as well as ice cream. Makers Liviko also produce a Vana Tallinn cream (⌨ www.liviko.ee).

Where to Eat

Tallinn has restaurants serving all kinds of international cuisine as well as Estonian dishes. The city has also been at the forefront of a revolution that has, in recent years, seen more and more ethnic restaurants opening in Estonia. Today you can dine in everything from Greek to Argentinian restaurants, as well as fast-food outlets, cafés, pizzerias, medieval-themed restaurants and some bars and nightclubs.

Food for a Special Occasion
Food and drink are integral to Estonian celebrations, with many of the country's festivals rooted in folk traditions. Celebratory foods include *sült* (jellied meat) served with hot mustard and potatoes, roast pork, goose, sauerkraut and *verivorst* (blood sausages). These also form part of the traditional Christmas meal. Lashings of beer, sweet wine and potent vodka help any celebration on its way.

All You Can Eat
If you are travelling on a budget and haven't had a good feed for a while then consider dining in one of Tallinn's buffet-style restaurants. Far superior to your British-style Chinese or pizza buffet experience, these include the **Park Avenue** at the swanky Reval Park Hotel and Casino (✉ Kreutzwaldi 23, ☎ 630 5305) and the equally swish **Tallink City Buffet and Restaurant** at the Hotel Tallink (✉ A. Laikmaa 5, ☎ 630 0800). More modest is the lunchtime soup buffet at the Reval Inn's **Express Café** (*see* page 58).

Above: *Staff at Olde Hansa restaurant wear medieval costume while serving hearty food.*

Old Town
• *LUXURY*
Stenhus

Feast on top-quality Estonian and international food at what is arguably the best restaurant in the Baltic States. Succulent scallops, langoustines cooked to perfection and tender fillet steak are just some of the mouthwatering dishes on offer. For a culinary treat opt for one of the chef's surprise tasting menus and choose between four, six and nine courses. Atmospheric cellar surrounds and first-rate service make the hefty price tag worthwhile. If you want to splash out on one great meal on your trip, make it here. ✉ *Pühavaimu 13/15*, ☎ *699 7700*.

Egoist

If you want to dine in this perennially popular restaurant you will need to book in advance. Fabulous cooking and a great wine list are the key components of Egoist's winning formula. Caviar, foie gras, lobster carpaccio and lamb are among the restaurant's expensive delights. ✉ *Vene 33*, ☎ *646 4052*.

Mookkala

If you love your seafood then this is the place for you. Feast on the likes of fresh eel, perch or salmon, with both local seafood and flown-in options on offer. More exotic dishes include swordfish and shark,

though carnivores are also catered for with decent fillet steaks and chateaubriand. The décor works well too, classy without being overblown, leaving it to the food to do the talking.
✉ *Kuninga 4,*
☎ *641 8288.*

Restaurant Margarita

A real treat in the heart of the Old Town. Head to the Barons Hotel and enjoy starters of the likes of caviar or snails, and then move on to grilled perch or wild boar. A good range of desserts to complete an ideal and pleasantly old-school dinner.
✉ *Suur-Karja 7,*
☎ *699 9705.*

Gloria

They don't get much better than Gloria. This fine-dining oasis serves up every bit as cultured a meal as you will find in most top-end places in London,

Rome or Paris. It more than deserves the various awards that have been flung its way. See for yourself in a blow-out where your contented glow afterwards is usually enough to assuage any financial guilt from which you might be suffering.
✉ *Müürivahe 2,*
☎ *644 6950.*

• *MID-RANGE*

Silk

Japanese cuisine is all the rage in the Baltics at the moment and there is no finer place in the region to sample some top-notch Japanese treats than in Silk. Feast on fresh sushi and sashimi in the heart of the Old Town. They also do a variety of maki dishes, including some excellent spicy options. You can also order the likes of miso soup, a range of hot dishes and Japanese beer. They now have another branch outside the Old Town at Narva mnt 15.

Popular with the city's beautiful people, these stylish sushi restaurants are places to see and be seen.
✉ *Kullasepa 4,*
☎ *648 4625.*

Pegasus

Drink with the in-crowd in the ground floor bar or make your way upstairs to enjoy sumptuous and innovative world cuisine. A refreshingly different menu conjures up fusion treats like whisky-cured salmon, blue cheese and prawn salad, spicy Malaysian laksa and roasted pheasant. From the minimalist dining room you can also soak up the view over St Nicholas's Church.
✉ *Harju 1,*
☎ *631 4040.*

KN Brasserie

Funky cellar brasserie in the Old Town that opened in 2005 and has become a firm favourite of the local cognoscenti. There's good service, large portions and plenty of atmosphere.

✉ *Dunkri 6, Merchant's House Hotel,* ☎ 697 7500.

Vanaema Juures

'Grandma's Place' is a wonderfully traditional and cosy old eatery that specializes in tasty local cooking, just like the Estonian grandmother you probably never had used to make it.

✉ *Rataskaevu 10/12,* ☎ 626 9080.

Turg

An Estonian-theme restaurant that tries to bring back a little bit of the country into the city as it slips back through the centuries. Decent traditional Estonian and 'Eastern European' food brightens up this cellar retreat.

✉ *Mundi 3,* ☎ 641 2456.

Olde Hansa

Enjoy a slice of medieval Tallinn at this restaurant, where staff don the cos-

tumes of a bygone era and litres of hoppy beer help ease the hearty meat dishes on their way.

✉ *Vana turg 1,* ☎ 627 9020.

• *BUDGET*
Von Krahl

Cheap and cheerful food is served up by equally cheerful staff. A local favourite are the large pancakes, which are a meal in themselves. Stay on for live music later on (*see page 76*).

✉ *Rataskaevu 10/12,* ☎ 626 9096.

Kompressor

If you like crepes you have come to the right place. All sorts of savoury and sweet options are on offer here, so tuck in for a budget treat that will fill you up before another bout of sightseeing.

✉ *Rataskaevu 3,* ☎ 646 4210.

Kumanets

This new Ukrainian restaurant is refresh-

ingly plain and simple and one of the increasingly few budget options in the Old Town. Traditional dumplings and pancakes sit happily on the menu alongside caviar and rabbit stew. Bacon fat in chocolate is a strange 'temptation' from the dessert menu.

✉ *Vene 8,* ☎ 525 5569.

Outside the Old Town
• *LUXURY*
Admiral

The maritime-theme décor in this old steamship might be the wrong side of kitsch but it sort of works, especially as you have a view of the harbour through the old portholes. The traditional Estonian cooking and meat grills are fine rather than amazing, but it is certainly one of the most unusual dining experiences in the city.

✉ *Lootsi 15,* ☎ 662 3777.

• *Mid-range*
Gianni

In a city now relatively replete with Italian restaurants this is one of the best. Ease into your candelit table and settle in for some fine Tuscan wine, fresh pasta and rich alcohol-infused desserts. More funky new Tallinn than Old Town charm, but still quite a romantic retreat.
✉ Joe 4a,
☎ 626 3684.

Eesti Maja

This is an understated Estonian restaurant that real Estonians would actually be seen in. There are few medieval frills here, just solid traditional cooking and plenty of hearty dishes – ideal when you are hungry after a hard day's sightseeing.
✉ Lauteri 1,
☎ 645 5252.

Paat

Worth a trip out of the centre for some seriously good cooking and some unusual architecture. The restaurant's name translates as 'boat', fitting as it actually looks like a capsized boat and it is in a beachside suburb. Seasonality here means sun-worshippers in summer lazing around on the beach and icebergs crunching up in front of you in winter.
✉ Rohuneeme tee 53,
☎ 609 0838.

• *Budget*
Narva Kohvik

Masochists and Cold War romantics can drift back through the years in this modest café/bakery haunt. Not so much retro chic as just plain old Soviet. A timewarp that is worth visiting once just for the sake of contrast.
✉ Narva 10,
☎ 660 1786.

Express Café

For business types on a budget, this is ideal as they offer free wireless access as well as a lunch soup buffet. Choose from one of the five savoury options and enjoy the sweet soup to finish. Perfect on a chilly Tallinn day and unbeatable for value with soup and a surf for less than the cost of a sandwich in the Old Town.
✉ Sadama 1,
☎ 667 8700.

Below: *Vanaema Juures, known as 'Grandma's Place', serves tasty traditional Estonian home cooking in a cosy setting.*

ENTERTAINMENT

Music Venues
Estonian National Opera
✉ Estonia pst 4
☎ 683 1214
💻 www.opera.ee
House of the Brotherhood of Blackheads
✉ Pikk 26
☎ 631 3199
💻 www.must peademaja.ee
St Nicholas's Church
✉ Niguliste 3
☎ 631 4330
💻 www.ekm.ee
Estonian Concert Hall
✉ Estonia pst 4
☎ 614 7700
💻 www.concert.ee
Linnahall
✉ Mere pst 20
☎ 641 1600
💻 www.linnahall.ee
Saku suurhall
✉ Paldiski mnt 104B
☎ 660 0200
💻 www.saku suurhall.ee

ENTERTAINMENT
Nightlife

In recent years, as non-residents have discovered Tallinn's nocturnal charms, the Estonian capital has become something of a party destination. This compact city is awash with bars and clubs that keep their doors open well into the night and often right through to the early hours of the morning.

For visitors in search of less raucous nightlife, Tallinn's Old Town streets are also flooded with cafés, many of which stay open till 23:00. Well over a dozen theatres, concert halls and cinemas are on hand to entertain those seeking a more cultural experience. A number of bars and clubs also host live gigs, with everything from rock and blues to funk and punk on offer.

Bars and Clubs

For the younger generation of locals and visitors Tallinn's nightlife scene revolves around thumping music, crowded bars and alcohol. One element, which accounts at least in part for Tallinn's growing popularity with partying tourists, are the comparatively low drink prices. Compared to Western European prices beer is cheap and myriad drinks promotions help to keep the cost of other alcoholic beverages down. Don't let this set alarm bells ringing, though, as not all of Tallinn's pubs are raucous watering holes where punters are primarily driven by price and a desire to get drunk. Instead, the Estonian capital boasts everything from chic lounge-style hangouts with live DJs, comfy couches and funky visuals, right through to bars, seemingly untouched for decades, frequented by older men.

70

In the business district the Radisson SAS (*see* page 57) is home to one of the city's coolest venues, **Lounge 24**; panoramic views of the Tallinn skyline from inside the bar and its terrace are spectacular.

In summer Tallinn's historic Old Town is the most atmospheric place to enjoy a tipple, as locals and visitors alike mingle over a hoppy Estonian brew at one of the many tables that have spilled out from the city's bars onto the largely pedestrianized streets. Here the obvious drinking choice is one of the pavement terraces of the bars and restaurants that flank **Rajeoka plats** (Town Hall Square).

Tallinn also has its fair share of adult entertainment venues (*see* panel, page 74). Popular with stag groups and businessmen, strippers, pole dancers and private lap dances are all part of the mix. Beware of hidden charges like expensive drinks for the dancers and prices that change according to how drunk you appear. Some clubs are more reputable than others.

Music

Whether you want to listen to a pop or a classical concert, Tallinn has live music venues to suit every taste. For an experience to remember book tickets for an operatic or ballet performance at the **Estonian National Opera**, the city's most esteemed venue. Other memorable places to listen to music traditionally associated with high culture include the **House of the Brotherhood of Blackheads** (*see* pages 20–21) and **St Nicholas's Church** (*see* pages 22–23).

Tallinn's principal classical music venue, though, is the **Estonian Concert Hall**, while

<u>**Children's Theatre**</u>
The **Estonian Puppet Theatre** has been engaging audiences of children since 1952. Today the **Eesti nukuteater** (Estonian Puppet Theatre) still uses puppetry in its shows, but children's plays and concerts also grace the stage. A puppet show can be engaging even if you don't understand the language being spoken by the puppeteers.
✉ Lai 1
☎ 667 9595
🖥 www.nukuteater.ee

Above: *The Estonian Concert Hall is the main venue for classical music concerts.*

Theatres
Estonian Drama Theatre
✉ Pärnu mnt 5
☎ 680 5555
💻 www.draama teater.ee
City Theatre
✉ Lai 2
☎ 665 0800,
💻 www.linnateater.ee
Von Krahl Theatre
✉ Ratsakaevu 10
☎ 626 9090
💻 www.vonkrahl.ee
Theatre NO99
✉ Salkala 3
☎ 660 5051
💻 www.no99.ee
Russian Theatre
✉ Vabaduse väljak 5
☎ 611 4911
💻 www.veneteater.ee

the **Linnahall** and **Saku suurhall** have the capacity to host famous bands from around the world. If rock and pop music played in intimate surrounds are more your thing, you can pay a visit to one of the numerous Tallinn hostelries that have regular live music (*see page 76*).

Theatre

The striking Art Nouveau Eesti draamateater (**Estonian Drama Theatre**), situated just southeast of the Old Town on Pärnu mnt, has been bringing dramatic productions to Tallinn since 1910. The mainly Estonian-language plays may not be to everyone's taste, but the theatre is worth visiting for the venue alone.

Non-Estonian speakers are more likely to find themselves at the Rahvusooper Estonia (**Estonian National Opera**), where the busy programme of ballet and opera runs alongside children's theatre and the occasional classical concert.

Alternative venues include the perennially popular Linnateater (**City Theatre**), with its resident group of actors, **Theatre NO99**, which hosts both foreign and Estonian contemporary drama, and the **Von Krahl Theatre**, an independent playhouse that prides itself on its cutting-edge productions. Tallinn also has a theatre geared towards the city's Russian community, where plays are performed in the Russian language; as you might expect this is called the Vene teater (**Russian Theatre**).

Cafés
Anneli Viik Handmade Chocolate Café

If you need some sugar to set you up for the night ahead, go to Anneli Viik. This wickedly indulgent café sells a mouth-watering range of handmade pralines, soft-centred choco-lates and truffles. It also serves light meals, cakes, teas, coffees and alcoholic drinks. Take away a souvenir box of chocolates.
✉ *Lai 6, Old Town,*
☎ *645 9017.*

Moskva

Not only does it sell rich coffees and snacks, but one of Tallinn's trendiest cafés also serves cock-tails and has live DJ sets. At night the sec-ond floor is the place to be. Southern fringe of the Old Town.
✉ *Vadabuse väljak 10,* ☎ *640 4694.*

La Bonaparte

Housed in an attrac-tive 17th-century building, La Bonaparte is a classic café where drinks are strictly non-alcoholic. This is a great place to grab a breakfast pastry, salad or quiche. Entering the café may take you back in time, but the hot drinks menu is decidedly modern, featuring the likes of café latte, oolong tea and even lemon rooibos.
✉ *Pikk 45, Old Town,*
☎ *646 4444.*

Café Peterson

Selling everything from coffee and fresh smoothies to hard liquor, Café Peterson is a good pit stop at any time of day. Admire the art in the attached gallery or enjoy live piano music at night. East of the Old Town.
✉ *Narva mnt 15,*
☎ *662 2195.*

Kehrwieder Café & Chocolaterie

Thanks to its Old Town Square location Kehrwieder is one of

Wi-Fi

One of the biggest surprises for many first-time visitors to the Estonian capital is the fact that Tallinn has definitely embraced the 21st century, which is great when it comes to checking your email and surfing the world-wide web. Myriad cafés, and increasingly bars, have wireless routers and all you need to do to log on is buy an access card from the counter staff. A growing number of cafés are even offering free Wi-Fi. So if you have got your own lap-top then you shouldn't have too many prob-lems finding some-where to get online.

ENTERTAINMENT

Adult Entertainment

The Can-Can Room is a reasonably reputable place on the southern fringes of the Old Town. Meanwhile, Mata Hari, on the same street, transforms into a strip club at 21:00. The sophisticated X Club and Mirtake are also located within the Old Town. Just outside the Old Town, Soho strives to attract the high-paying business clientele that stay in the nearby Radisson SAS hotel.

Can-Can Room
✉ Suur-Karja 10
☎ 683 5205

Mata Hari
✉ Suur-Karja 11
☎ 631 4900

X Club
✉ Harju 6
☎ 631 0575
💻 www.xclub.ee

Mirtake
✉ Väike-Karja 1
☎ 644 3006
💻 www.mirtake.ee

Soho
✉ Kaubamaja 3
☎ 681 4616
💻 www.soho.ee

Opposite: *Saku is one of the most popular of Estonian beers and is served in bars, cafés and restaurants across the city.*

Tallinn's busiest cafés. To really appreciate it you'll have to go inside. If you are feeling peckish there are cakes and pastries to choose from, as well as salads and sandwiches.

✉ *Saiakang 1, Old Town.*

Bars and Pubs
Nimeta Baar

Believe it or not, the Tartan Army (the nickname given to fans of Scotland's national football team) breathed new life into Tallinn's sluggish nightlife back in the 1990s, staying behind after a football match to set up two bars. The Nimeta Baar and the Nimega Baar (*see this page*) are still going strong. Big screen sports, pub grub and live DJ sets ensure the popularity of the British-style Nimeta Baar (The Pub with No Name) with locals, tourists and expatriates alike.

✉ *Suur-Karja 4, Old Town,* ☎ *641 1515.*

Nimega Baar

The name of the Nimeta Baar's sister pub translates as (you've guessed it) The Pub with a Name. Like the Nimeta, Nimega is a good place to meet locals keen to practise their English. Cheap drinks promotions and a throbbing dance floor are just two of the attractions at this lively bar. During the day you can use their wireless Internet free of charge.

✉ *Suur-Karja 13, Old Town,* ☎ *620 9299.*

Molly Malone's

Not only does this above average Irish-themed pub boast a great location, but it has regular live music and screens big sporting matches. Then of course there is Guinness and Kilkenny on tap and a range of speciality ciders. In the summer months the action spills out onto its Town Hall Square terrace.

✉ *Mundi 2, Old Town,* ☎ *631 3016.*

BARS AND PUBS

Kaheksa

Premium drink prices, wealthy slightly older clientele and a tropical theme lend Kaheksa a sophisticated air. This lounge bar is one of the most fashionable in Tallinn and a place to see and be seen, so dress to impress.
✉ Vana-Posti 8, Old Town, ☎ 627 4770.

Pegasus

This trendy fusion eatery (see page 67) is home to an equally stylish bar. Champagne cocktails are the way to go, just don't expect them to be cheap.
✉ Harju 1, Old Town, ☎ 631 4040.

Beer House

The privilege of supping a beer brewed by Tallinn's only microbrewery comes at a price, namely the German oompah bands and the raucous groups of drunk (mainly male) tourists. Pop into this Bavarian-style beer hall earlier in the day for a more serene drinking expe-

rience. Drinks are at their cheapest during the very early happy hour (12:00–14:00 daily). If you plan to drink until you drop then you can also line your stomach with the likes of roast chicken, sausages, pizza and deep-fried cheese.
✉ Dunkri 5, Old Town, ☎ 644 222.

Bar Bogart

If you are after a bit of light-hearted fun then this Humphrey Bogart theme bar at the Sokos Hotel Viru could be for you. The bar pumps out dance music earlier in the evening before switching to karaoke (generally 21:00–

Beer House Brews

Tallinn's only micro-brewery, the Beer House, sells seven of its own brand drinks. The **Pilsner Gold** is a light-coloured lager with an alcohol content of around 4.5%. Then there is the **Märzen Speziel**, another lager beer with a red tinge and full flavour. Again, its alcohol content is around 4.5%. The **Dunkles Extra** (4.6–4.8%), mean-while, is a dark beer with a mellow and slightly sweet taste. **Helles Light** is a good choice for those who prefer a sweeter lager, although it is decep-tively strong at 4.9%. Sweeter still is the **Medovar Honey** beer (4.3–4.5%). For a full-bodied dark beer, plump for **Vana Viini** (4.7–5.0%); finally there is the strong (5.0–5.3%) **BH Premium**.

01:00), then back to the disco before closing at 03:00 (11:00 on Monday). Don't come on a Sunday though as the bar is closed. ✉ *Sokos Hotel Viru, Viru väljak 4,* ☎ *680 9300.*

Stereo Lounge

Taking white minimalism to its extremes, the Stereo Lounge is currently considered very cool. Live DJ sets and chilled house music and a cocktail list that runs to 60 different drinks keep the local in-crowd happy. The lively menu covers everything from a light breakfast omelette to tasty wraps, salads and rich chocolate cake. Where any resemblance to a stereo lies, though, is a mystery. ✉ *Harju 6, Old Town,* ☎ *631 0549.*

X-Baar

See page 44.

Live Music
Kolumbus
Krisostomus

The Christopher

Columbus bar is a venue for those who don't take themselves too seriously, with regular Salsa and karaoke nights. The rest of this beer-hall-style pub's diary is dotted with promising new local bands. ✉ *Viru 24,* ☎ *5615 6924 (mobile).*

Rock Café

Tallinn's best rock club is housed in a former factory close to the main bus station. Weekend nights are generally booked up with live acts and not just unknown ones either. Recent performers include Fish (the former front man of Marillion), WASP and Uriah Heep. ✉ *Tartu mnt 80d,* 🖥 *www.rockcafe.ee*

Scotland Yard

This large pub on the way to the port can be a lively place at any time. Internally it is supposed to look like a police station, but with a wall of old books it is closer to a

library. Aside from decent pub food and a large selection of drinks the main reason to come here is to hear a rock band. Gigs are usually free and tend to be held on a Thursday, Friday or Saturday nights. ✉ *Mere pst 6e,* ☎ *653 5190.*

Von Krahl

Wi-Fi, cheap food and a young artsy crowd make Von Krahl a popular daytime haunt with Tallinn's student population. This is also the place to come to see a band if you prefer music of the alternative kind. The bar is part of the Von Krahl Theatre (see page 72). ✉ *Rataskaevu 10/12,* ☎ *626 9096.*

Martini Jazz Café

There may be nothing that particularly stands out about this small, minimalist bar, but for jazz fans this newcomer on Tallinn's nightlife scene is your best bet. When live

acts are on the place fills up quickly so arrive early, especially if you want a seat.
✉ Väike-Karja 1, ☎ 5330 0002 (mobile).

Café Amigo
See below.

Nightclubs
Café Amigo
When it comes to nightlife it seems that the Sokos Hotel Viru can do no wrong. Early on the dance floor fills with a mixture of tourists and locals who have come to dance to retro tunes from the 70s, 80s and 90s. Later in the evening blues and rock bands regularly take to the stage.
✉ Sokos Hotel Viru, Viru väljak 4, ☎ 680 9300.

Hollywood
This Old Town club is popular with backpackers and Tallinn's younger revellers. A steady diet of dance music, go-go dancers and assorted raised stages make it a fun place. Wednesday

night is ladies' night when the club basically turns into a pick-up joint.
✉ Vana-Posti 8, Old Town, ☎ 627 4770.

BonBon
This exclusive club located down near the port is only open on Wednesdays, Fridays and Saturdays, when the doors stay open until 05:00. With an above-average admission price and stylish interior, BonBon really is a place to see and be seen, so dress to impress. If it is really busy the bouncers tend to turn non-members away.
✉ Mere pst 6e, ☎ 661 6080.

Bonnie & Clyde
If you want to boogie away from the hordes of teenagers that throng Tallinn's Old Town nightclubs then you could do worse than Bonnie & Clyde. It may be located in a hotel, but the Reval Hotel Olümpia's night-

club is actually one of the city's most popular, attracting a more mature crowd. South of the Old Town.
✉ Liivalaia 33, ☎ 631 5333.

Privé
Another trendy Old Town club with great live DJ sets. The quality, though, isn't always consistent and a visit here can be a bit hit and miss.
✉ Harju 6, Old Town, ☎ 631 0545.

Angel
See page 44.

Below: *The interior of Stereo Lounge is minimalist, the menu varied, and the cocktail list extensive.*

EXCURSIONS

EXCURSIONS

Away from Tallinn a different Estonia starts to appear. Gone are the gleaming office blocks and smooth business hotels and in their place are old wooden houses, crumbling castle ruins and sweeping lakes, as the centuries seem to peel back at every turn.

Above: *The ruins of Tartu Cathedral are much visited.*

Tartu
Location: Map D–D2
Distance from city: 180km (112 miles)
Tartu Tourist Information, ✉ Raekoja plats 14, ☎ 744 2111, 🖥 www.visittartu.com
Raekoda, ✉ Raekoja plats
Tartu University, ✉ Ülikooli 18, 🖥 www.ut.ee
Jaani kirik, ✉ Jaani 5, ☎ 744 2229, 🖥 www.jaanikirik.ee ⏰ 10:00–18:00 Tue–Sat.

Viljandi
Location: Map D–D2
Distance from city: 160km (99 miles)
Viljandi Tourist Information, ✉ Vabaduse plats 6, ☎ 433 0442, 🖥 www.viljandimaa.ee
Viljandi muuseum, ✉ Kindral Laidoneri plats 10, ☎ 433 3316, 🖥 www.muuseum.viljandimaa.ee ⏰ 10:00–17:00 Wed–Sun.

Tartu

This vibrant university city, home to more than 15,000 students, is the second largest in Estonia, and well worth a visit. Habitation of the area has been traced back to the 6th century AD, though Tartu didn't appear in written records until 1030. Since then it has been ruled by German, Russian, Polish, Lithuanian and Swedish occupiers.

Tartu's sights include the central **Raekoja plats (Town Hall Square)**, its neoclassical **University** building, and the elaborate façade of the Gothic **Jaani kirik (St John's Church)**. In addition to historic buildings, Tartu also boasts over a dozen museums.

Viljandi

Despite a turbulent history that has seen it ravaged by fire, as well Russian, German, Swedish and Polish armies, Viljandi still has a number of interesting sights. The most obvious is the omnipresent crumbling 13th-century **Livonian Order Castle**, which opens up a panoramic view over **Lake Viljandi**.

A neo-Renaissance **courthouse**, an 18th-century **town hall**, **suspension bridge** and **water tower** all number amongst Viljandi's attractions, as do the **Viljandi muuseum**

78

(**Viljandi Museum**), the neo-Renaissance **Viljandi mõis** (**Viljandi Manor**) and a couple of handsome churches.

Rakvere

Founded in 1252, Rakvere boasts two well-known sights: its partially ruined medieval **Rakvere linnus** (**Rakvere Castle**) and the **Tarvas statue**. The work of Estonian sculptor Tauno Kangro, the latter is an oversized auroch (European bison), which the city proudly proclaims is the largest statue of an animal in the Baltic States. The town is also home to striking churches, **Rakvere linnakodaniku majamuuseum** (**Rakvere Citizen's Museum**), an old wooden house whose interior sheds light on early 20th-century life in the city, and **Rakvere näitusemaja** (**Rakvere Exhibition House**), which has served as a bank and prison since its construction towards the end of the 18th century.

Väike-Maarja

Culturally rich Väike-Maarja is a worthwhile diversion. Located in a former schoolhouse (constructed in 1869), the **Väike-Maarja muuseum** (**Väike-Maarja Museum**) focuses on local history and the awakening of a national consciousness in the region. **Kiltsi loos** (**Kiltsi Castle**) is a striking 18th-century Baltic-German manor estate. The **Vao tornlinnus-muuseum** (**Vao Stronghold Tower Museum**) harks back to the early 14th century, when lookout towers like this were dotted all over Estonia.

Paldiski

A former Soviet naval base, Paldiski, located 45km (30 miles) west of Tallinn, was once

Rakvere
Location: Map D–D1
Distance from city: 100km (62 miles)
Rakvere Tourist Information, ✉ Laada 14, ☎ 324 2734, 🖥 www.rakvere.ee
Rakvere linnus, ✉ Vallimägi, ☎ 322 5500, 🖥 www.svm.ee
Rakvere linnakodaniku majamuuseum, ✉ Pikk 50, ☎ 324 4248, 🖥 www.svm.ee ⏰ 10:00–17:00 Thu–Sat, closed Sun–Wed.
Rakvere näitusemaja, ✉ Tallinna 3, ☎ 322 5500, 🖥 www.svm.ee ⏰ 10:00–17:00 Thu–Sat, closed Sun–Wed.

Väike-Maarja
Location: Map D–D1
Distance from city: 130km (81 miles)
Väike-Maarja Tourist Information, ✉ Pikk 3, ☎ 326 1625, 🖥 www.v-maarja.ee
Väike-Maarja muuseum, ✉ Pikk 3, ☎ 326 1625, 🖥 www.v-maarja.ee ⏰ 10:00–17:00 Tue–Sat, closed Sun & Mon (May–Sep); 10:00–17:00 Mon–Fri, closed Sat & Sun (Oct–Apr).
Kiltsi loos, ☎ 325 3411, ⏰ 08:00–13:00 Mon & Tue, 08:00–19:00 Wed–Fri, 11:00–19:00 Sat & Sun.
Vao tornlinnus-muuseum, ☎ 326 625, ⏰ 11:00–18:00 Wed–Sun, closed Mon & Tue (May–Aug).

one of the busiest ports in the Russian Empire. Established by Peter the Great in 1718, it became a naval base in 1939 and, later, a training ground for the crew of the USSR's nuclear submarines. Abandoned in 1994, a collection of run-down and derelict buildings provide an insight into the military might that propped up the old Iron Curtain (at one time more than 16,000 military personnel were based here).

Paldiski
Location: Map D–C1
Distance from city:
45km (30 miles)

Peipsi Järve
Location: Map D–E2
Distance from city:
250km (155 miles)

National Parks
Estonia's smallest national park, **Karula** (⌨ www.karularahvus park.ee), boasts an attractive landscape of meadow, forest, lakes and bogs. For visitors this translates as a tranquil environment for walking, swimming and fishing, as well as berry/mushroom picking (with a guide). The landscape of **Soomaa National Park** (⌨ www.soomaa.ee) is characterized by thick forest, flat marshy flood plains and rivers. It is also home to many animal and bird species, including beavers, otters, waterfowl, eagles and wolves.

Lake Peipsi

The biggest lake in Estonia and the fourth-largest body of water in Europe, **Peipsi järv (Lake Peipsi)** is actually located in both Estonia and the Russian Federation; the latter owns the greatest share (56%). This has practical implications for fishermen who need to ensure that they don't stray into Russian-owned water by mistake. Relatively undisturbed by tourism (even Estonians don't really come here), the surface area of the lake is a whopping 3555km^2 (1373 sq miles) and those who make the effort to visit are rewarded by tranquil woodland and quiet sandy beaches. Winter transforms the warm and bathing waters into an icy wasteland.

Lahemaa Rahvuspark

Established in 1971 and spanning an area of 725km^2 (280 sq miles) – 474 km^2 (183 sq miles) on land and 251km^2 (97 sq miles) of sea – Lahemaa is both the largest and the oldest national park in Estonia.

Situated about 80km (50 miles) from Tallinn, this conservation area boasts tranquil villages (like Viinistu, Käsmu, Võsu and Altja), old wooden houses, a couple of museums, ancient woodlands, peat bogs and a coastline dotted with erratic boulders. The relaxed pace of life and the 'getting away from it all' feeling are Lahemaa's main drawcards.

The architectural highlight of the park is the 19th-century **Palmse mõis (Palmse Manor)**, which is heralded as one of the most attractive Baltic-German estates in this part of Europe. Palmse boasts woodland walks, a swan lake and an exhibition of old motor vehicles.

The **Lahemaa National Park Visitor Centre** is also located within the manor, and there is a café, hotel and restaurant on site.

Haapsalu

Balmy sea water, an attractive seaside promenade and curative mud have ensured the popularity of Haapsalu with Estonian holiday-makers over the decades. For most foreign visitors **Haapsalu loss (Haapsalu Episcopal Castle)**, one of Estonia's best-preserved castles, and its integral cathedral, **Toom-Niguliste Kirik (St Nicholas's Dome Church)**, are the principal reasons for visiting this 13th-century settlement. More than a historic relic, the castle is still used for open-air events.

Lahemaa Rahvuspark
Location: Map D–D1
Distance from city: 50km (31 miles)
Palmse mõis, ⊠ Palmse, ☎ 324 0070, 🖳 www.svm.ee ⏱ 10:00–16:00 Tue–Sat, closed Sun & Mon (Oct–Apr); daily 10:00–19:00 (May–Sep).
Lahemaa National Park Visitor Centre, ⊠ Palmse, ☎ 329 5555, 🖳 www.lahemaa.ee ⏱ 09:00–17:00 Mon–Fri, closed Sat & Sun.

Haapsalu
Location: Map D–B2
Distance from city: 100km (62 miles)
Haapsalu Tourist Information, ⊠ Posti 37, ☎ 473 3248, 🖳 www.haapsalu.ee

Opposite: *Lahemaa National Park.*
Below: *Haapsalu's historical castle.*

Above: *The Angla windmills at Saaremaa, Estonia's largest island.*

Pärnu
Location: Map D–C2
Distance from city:
130km (81 miles)
Pärnu Tourist
Information, ✉ Rüütli
16, ☎ 447 3000, 🖥
www.visitparnu.com
Raekoda, ✉ Uss
4/Nikolai 3
Ekateriina kirik,
✉ Vee 16
Issandamuutmise
kirik, ✉ Aia 5
Eliisabeti kirik,
✉ Nikolai 22

Pärnu

Sandy beaches and a lively nightlife (in season) have helped establish Pärnu as Estonia's main seaside resort. Pavement cafés, decent restaurants and increasingly sophisticated hotels back up its tourist industry. Whatever the season this old Hanseatic city is also popular with people seeking curative spa therapies (something that it has been offering since the first facility opened in 1838) or just a relaxing massage.

Since the city's history can be traced back over 11,000 years, there is more to Pärnu than beaches and spa hotels. Downtown highlights include the Classicist **Raekoda (Town Hall)**, the Baroque masterpiece that is **Ekateriina kirik (St Catherine's Church)**, the **Issandamuutmise kirik (Transfiguration of The Lord Orthodox Church**, finished in 1904) and neo-Gothic **Eliisabeti kirik (Elizabeth Church)**.

Several important monuments and fortifications also dot Pärnu, with the former prison tower – the **Punane torn (Red Tower)** – which forms part of the 15th-century town walls, the 17th-century **Tallinna värav (Tallinn Gate)** and the **Munamägi** defensive bastions being among the most impressive.

A wealth of historic and architecturally distinct houses dating from the 16th–20th centuries, grandiose public buildings and banks, museums, galleries and theatres complete Pärnu's rich cultural fabric.

Saaremaa

Saaremaa is Estonia's largest island and has been inhabited for at least 5000 years. Key sights include the main and historic settlement of **Kuressaare** and the **Angla tuulikud (Angla Windmills)**; they may be the only surviving cluster of windmills on the island, but at one time these could be found outside every village. Today five of the nine original windmills are still standing.

Elsewhere, the **Kaali kraater (Kaali Crater)**, a circular lake created almost 3000 years ago, and **Vilsandi rahvuspark (Vilsandi National Park)** also merit a visit. Driving around Saaremaa you will also come across appealing churches, 17th- and 18th-century manor houses, forest, ancient and ruined fortifications, attractive bays, lakes, sheer cliff faces, sacrificial springs, lighthouses and nature reserves.

Hiiumaa

An island that has yet to really embrace the 21st century, it is Hiiumaa's unspoilt nature and unhurried pace of life that attracts savvy holiday-makers. From the 13th-century church (Hiiumaa's oldest) at **Pühalepa** and a couple of handsome lighthouses to the faded grandeur of **Suure-mõisa mõis (Suuremõisa Manor)** and the **Hiiumaa muuseum (Hiiumaa Museum)** just outside Kassari, the island does have a number of sights.

Most visitors, however, come to watch the birds at the **Käina Bay Bird Reserve**, to soak up the fine coastal views, or to simply walk and cycle on this peaceful island. The island's capital, **Kärdla**, is a pleasant place with green parks and woodland.

Saaremaa
Location: Map D–A2
Distance from city:
170km (105 miles)
🖥 www.saaremaa.ee
Kuressaare Tourist Information
✉ Tallinna 2
☎ 453 3120
🖥 www.kuressaare.ee
Angla tuulikud
✉ on the Upa-Leisi road
Kaali kraater,
✉ Kaali
Vilsandi rahvuspark
🖥 www.vilsandi.ee

Hiiumaa
Location: Map D–B2
Distance from city:
135km (84 miles)
Hiiumaa Tourist Information
✉ Hiiu 1, Kärdla
☎ 462 232
🖥 www.hiiumaa.ee.
Hiiumaa muuseum
✉ Vabriku väljak 8, Kärdla
☎ 463 2091
🖥 www.muuseum.hiiumaa.ee
🕐 10:00–17:00 Mon–Fri, 11:00–14:00 Sat

Above: *Tourist information signs point the way in Tallinn, a city that is increasingly geared toward the needs of visitors.*

Road Signs

Road signs in Estonia are quite straightforward and should present no real problems to drivers who have not driven in the country before. On highways arrows with the destination name indicate which lane you should be in, similar signs are found at major junctions, and in some cases a road designation number is also shown. Mandatory speed limits are given inside a circle.

Best Times to Visit

Late spring and early autumn are probably the best times to visit Tallinn; the weather is mild and the number of tourists fewer, making conditions ideal for exploring the city on foot. While summer days can be hot, reaching the mid-20s (°C), temperatures are nowhere near as high as they are in southern Europe, so the tourist season (Jun–Aug) is a good time to visit, as long as you don't mind busier streets and inflated accommodation prices. In summer Tallinn also takes on a more Mediterranean feel as the tables and chairs move outside and alfresco drinking and dining is usual. Though daytime temperatures often fall below 0°C, the Estonian capital can be rewarding to visit in winter, with the chill daytime temperatures encouraging you to spend more time indoors, thoroughly exploring its museums, churches and other historic buildings. Bars, cafés, restaurants and clubs become the regular haunt of locals during winter, making a visit out of season often feel more authentic. Whenever you visit Tallinn there is a good chance of rain.

Tourist Information

The **Estonian Tourist Board** has offices in

Finland (Helsinki), Germany (Hamburg), the UK (London), Sweden (Stockholm) and Russia (St Petersburg).

Finland: ✉ Mariankatu 8B, 00170 Helsinki, ☎ (+358 9) 2289 0444, 📠 (+358 9) 2289 0445, 🖳 helsinki@eas.ee 🖳 www.visitestonia.com

Germany: ✉ Mönckebergstr 5, 20095 Hamburg, ☎ (+49 40) 3038 7899, 📠 (+49 40) 3038 7981, 🖳 hamburg@eas.ee 🖳 www.visitestonia.com

UK: ✉ 6 Hyde Park Gate, London SW7 5DG, ☎ (+44 020) 7838 5390, 📠 (+44 020) 7838 5391, 🖳 info@cnto.freeserve.co.uk or london@eas.ee 🖳 www.visitestonia.com

Sweden: ✉ Wallingatan 32, 2tr, 111 24 Stockholm, ☎ (+46 8) 236 018, 📠 (+46 8) 442 2080, 🖳 stockholm@eas.ee 🖳 www.visitestonia.com

Russia: ✉ Gorohovaja 3, 190000 St Petersburg, ☎ (+7 812) 103 7104, 📠 (+7 812) 103 7105, 🖳 st.petersburg@eas.ee 🖳 www.

visitestonia.com.
The **national tourist board** also has an office in Tallinn at: ✉ Liivalaia 13/15, ☎ (372) 627 9770, 📠 (372) 627 9777, 🖳 tourism@aes.ee 🖳 www.visitestonia.com

For German visitors the **Baltic Tourism Information Centre** is another source of information: ✉ Katharinenstr. 19-20, 10711 Berlin-Wilmersdorf, ☎ (49 30) 8900 9091, 📠 (49 30) 8900 9092, 🖳 info@baltikuminfo.de 🖳 www.baltikuminfo.de

The **Tallinn Tourist Board Information Centre** is located on the corner of Niguliste and Kullasepa at: ✉ Niguliste 2/Kullasepa 4, ☎ (372) 6457 777, 📠 (372) 6457 778, 🖳 turismiinfo@tallinnlv.ee 🖳 www.touirsm.tallinn.ee ⏰ 09:00–17:00 Mon–Fri, 10:00–15:00 Sat (Oct–Apr); 09:00–19:00 Mon–Fri, 10:00–17:00 Sat–Sun (May–Jun); 09:00–20:00 Mon–Fri, 10:00–18:00 Sat–Sun

(Jul–Aug); 09:00–18:00 Mon–Fri, 10:00–17:00 Sat–Sun (Sep).
There is another office in the city centre at: ✉ Viru väljak 4, ☎ (372) 610 1557 or (372) 610 1558, 📠 (372 610 1559), 🖳 turismi info@tallinnlv.ee 🖳 www.touirsm.tallinn.ee ⏰ 09:00–21:00.

Entry Requirements

Most visitors, including those from the European Union (EU) and European Economic Area (EEA), only need a valid passport or a National Identity Card to enter Estonia. Current visa regulations can be checked with the Ministry of Foreign Affairs (🖳 www.vm.ee). Estonia joined the Schengen Zone in December 2007; in principle this allows visitors to pass between Schengen countries without border checks.

Customs

Estonia is part of the EU, so there is no duty-free allowance for those travelling from another EU country. Consumer goods for personal use can be transported freely without incurring additional tax. Some restrictions, however, still apply. Visitors from within the EU are allowed to bring a maximum of 800 cigarettes, 400 cigarillos, 200 cigars, 1kg tobacco, 110 litres of beer, 90 litres of wine, 20 litres of liqueur, 10 litres of spirits, 10kg of coffee and 110 litres of non-alcoholic beverages. Visitors from outside the EU are permitted to bring 200 cigarettes or the equivalent, one litre of spirits or two litres of liqueur or wine, 50g of perfume, 250ml eau de toilette and new/unused items to the value of 175 euros into any of the three Baltic States without paying customs duty.

Health Requirements

You do not need any vaccinations to visit Estonia. EU citizens in possession of a European Health Insurance Card (EHIC) are entitled to free emergency health care in Estonia. Non-emergency treatment, prescriptions and repatriation costs, however, are not covered by the EHIC and all visitors should purchase full travel insurance.

Getting There

Tallinn is accessible by road, rail, sea and air.
By air: Tallinn International Airport (💻 www.tallinn-airport.ee) is located 4km (2.5 miles) from the city centre. A taxi into the centre takes 10–15 minutes depending on traffic. There are direct flights to Tallinn from Amsterdam, Brussels, Copenhagen, Frankfurt, Helsinki, London, Milan, Oslo, Prague, Riga, Salzburg, Stockholm, Vilnius and Warsaw, amongst other destinations. Airlines operating these routes include Estonian Air (💻 www.estonian-air.ee), Air Baltic (💻 www.airbaltic.com), Czech Airlines (💻 www.czechairlines.com), easyJet (💻 www.easyjet.com), Finnair (💻 www.finnair.com) and Lufthansa (💻 www.lufthansa.com).
By road: Estonia is bordered by Russia in the east and Latvia in the south. The city is connected to the rest of Estonia by a series of numbered highways. Where highways lead to other countries they have also been designated as European roads (these are indicated in brackets). Highway 1 (E20) heads east to Narva and the Russian border, while Highway 2 travels southeast to Tartu and onto the Russian border again. Heading south on Highway 4 (E67) takes you to Latvia via Pärnu. Highway 9 branches southwest in search of Haapsalu, it also meets Highway 10 to Virtsu. Highway 8 meanwhile heads west to Paldiski. Much of Tallinn's pedestrianized Old City is closed to private vehicles, which

can make finding a parking space a real pain. Driving around the rest of the city can be a hair-raising experience. Once you are outside of the capital driving around Estonia is relatively straightforward, although local drivers can be a bit reckless when it comes to overtaking on single-lane roads. If you bring your own car into the country a Green Card (international vehicle insurance) is necessary and third party insurance is compulsory. A valid national driving licence and in some instances an international driving licence is also required. Driving in Estonia is on the right. Hiring a car for a stay in Tallinn is not necessary as its key sights are easily navigable on foot and the city's public transport system is efficient. In order to hire a car, drivers must be over 21 with at least a year's (some companies specify two) driving experi-

ence. Seatbelts are compulsory, headlights must be turned on and blood alcohol may not exceed 0.02%. Speed limits are 50kph in built-up areas and 90kph on highways unless otherwise stated. In case of an emergency breakdown contact the **Automobile Club of Estonia**, ☎ 1888. If you are stopped by the police they will ask to see your passport/national ID card and driving licence, plus the car's registration and insurance documents. International buses (⌨ www.eurolines.com or www.ecolines.net) connect Tallinn to destinations throughout Europe, including Rīga, Hamburg, Kaliningrad, Kiev, Munich and St Petersburg. Numerous Estonian towns have direct buses to Tallinn. **Tallinn Bus Station** (☎ 12 550; ⌨ www.bussiriside.ee ☺ daily 05:00–24:00) is a good source of information. **By rail:** Direct international rail services (⌨ www.ldz.lv) run

Public Holidays
1 January • New Year's Day
24 February • Independence Day
March/April • Good Friday
March/April • Easter Sunday
1 May • Labour Day
23 June • Victory Day
24 June • Midsummer
20 August • Restoration of Independence
24–26 December • Christmas Holidays

<u>Good Reading</u>
O'Connor, Kevin (2003) *The History of the Baltic States.* Greenwood Press, Burnham.
Lieven, Anatol (1996) *The Baltic Revolution: Estonia, Latvia, Lithuania and the Path to Independence.* Yale University Press, London.
Smith, David (2002) *The Baltic States: Estonia, Latvia and Lithuania.* Routledge, Abingdon.
Mole, Richard (2008) *The Baltic States: From Soviet Union to European Union.* Routledge, Abingdon.

between Tallinn and St Petersburg. Domestic services link the capital to Tartu, Valga, Türi, Viljandi, Tapa, Narva and Pärnu. **Edelaraudette** (⌨ www.edel.ee) operate intercity services. The city's main train station is at ✉ Toompuiestee 37, ☎ 1444 or (372) 615 6851, ⌨ www.baltijaam.ee.

By sea: Tallinn can be reached by ferry from Helsinki (Finland), Stockholm (Sweden) and Rostock (Germany). Services are operated by **Tallink Estonia** (⌨ www.tallink.ee), **Eckerö Line** (☎ 372 664 6000, ⌨ www.eckeroline.ee), **Super Sea Cat** (☎ 372 610 0000, ⌨ www.super seacat.com), **Viking Line** (⌨ www.viking line.fi) and **Nordic Jet Line** (☎ 372 613 7000, ⌨ www.njl.ee).

What to Pack

Sun protection is essential in summer. In winter temperatures often plummet below 0°C. Casual clothing is acceptable almost everywhere, with smart casual for the more expensive restaurants. Business attire is formal. Other essentials include camera battery chargers/spare batteries, digital camera memory cards/camera film and plug adaptors. An umbrella or waterproof jacket might be needed at any time of year. Photocopy important documents and make a note of any prescription medicines that you are taking. Consider packing spare glasses and contact lenses.

Money Matters

Currency: Estonia's national currency is the Estonia kroon (EEK). There are 100 cents to the kroon.
Currency exchange: There are banks and exchange bureaux all over the city, some of which take overseas credit cards in their automatic tellers; banking hours are ⊕ 09:00–18:00 Mon–Fri,

10:00–15:00 Sat. Traveller's cheques can also be changed in banks and some travel agencies.

Credit cards: All major cards are accepted although some outlets may require cash. Holders of cards with the Visa, Mastercard, Maestro, Cirrus and American Express logos can often use Estonian ATMs, which generally have ir ructions in English. A fee is usually charged for this.

Sales tax: The standard rate of Value Added Tax is 18%.

Tipping: When it comes to tipping some restaurants automatically levy a 10% service charge. Where no service charge is indicated gratuities are optional; however it is courteous to leave 10–15%. If you buy a drink at the bar service is not expected.

Transport

Tallinn's Old City is easily navigable on foot. It also has an efficient network of city buses, trolleybuses and trams, which can be useful for travelling to sights or accommodation outside the historic centre. Tickets for public transport can be purchased from news kiosks or from the driver. Buying a ticket on board costs almost twice as much. Once on board you need to punch a hole in your ticket to validate it; failure to do so results in a fine if a ticket inspector catches you. Tallinn's taxis are reasonably cheap and can be hailed on the street or found at taxi ranks. Unscrupulous drivers sometimes try to overcharge tourists. Three things may help you avoid this: ensure that you only use a licensed taxi; insist that the meter is turned on; and pre-book your taxi by phone. Most drivers speak English, but it is still a good idea to write down the address of where you want to go just in case you need it.

Business Hours

Shops are generally open ⏰ 10:00–19:00 Mon–Fri and close slightly earlier on Saturdays. Shops are also increasingly open on Sundays. Supermarkets and shopping centres keep longer hours. Office hours meanwhile tend to be ⏰ 09:00–18:00 Mon–Fri. Post offices open ⏰ 08:00–20:00 Mon–Fri and 08:00–16:00 Sat, although some stay open until later. Banking hours are ⏰ 09:00–18:00 Mon–Fri and 10:00–15:00 Sat. Restaurants open from ⏰ 11:00–23:00 daily, although this may vary slightly and some open as early as ⏰ 07:00 for the breakfast trade. Most cafés open early (usually between ⏰ 08:00 and 10:00) and stay open until 22:00–24:00. Bars tend to open an hour or so before midday and keep serving drinks until at least ⏰ 24:00 during the week and 02:00 on

TRAVEL TIPS

Estonian Phrases
Tere • **hello**
Nägemiseni, nägemist •
goodbye
Palun • **please**
Täna, aitäh • **thank
you**
Kui palju? • **how
much?**
Haigla • **hospital**
Lennujaam • **airport**
Üks • **one**
Kaks • **two**
Kolm • **three**
Neli • **four**
Viis • **five**
Kuus • **six**
Seitse • **seven**
Kaheksa • **eight**
Üheksa • **nine**
Kümme • **10**
Sada • **100**

Eating Out
Cafés, snack bars, fast-food joints, traditional inns and restaurants cater to a wide range of budgets. Cuisine is influenced by geography and climate. With its roots in rural peasant culture, Estonian food tends to be 'hearty'. Estonia is where, in the Baltics, you are likely to find more salads and the culinary influences of Scandinavia creeping in. With a large swathe of Baltic coast, seafood is popular too, the highlights being herring and salmon. Vodka and local liqueur Vana Tallinn compete for popularity with beer, with the most renowned brewer of the latter being Saku.

Friday and Saturday nights. A lot stay open until much later. Nightclubs generally do not open until at least ☯ 20:00 (and they don't get going until much later) and run right through to around ☯ 05:00; many nightclubs are also closed at the beginning of the week.

Time Difference
Estonia is in the Eastern European Time Zone (EET). EET is GMT+2. The country also observes Daylight Saving. This means that from the last Sunday in March to the last Sunday in October it is GMT+2, for the rest of the time it is GMT+3.

Communications
Phone: The international dialling code for Estonia is ☎ +372. There are no area codes in Estonia. When calling Tallinn from overseas you need to dial the country code and then the full telephone num-

ber. To call overseas from the Estonian capital, dial ☎ 00 and wait for the tone to change before dialling the country code and the number. You can make a direct local, national or international call from any public telephone using a phone card (available from post offices and newspaper kiosks). Prepaid mobile phone cards are available from AS EMT (⌨ www.emt.ee), Elisa (⌨ www.elisa.ee) and Tele2 (⌨ www. tele2.ee).

Post: The Central Post Office is located at ✉ Narva mnt 1; ☯ open 07:30–20:00 Mon–Fri and 08:00–18:00 Sat.

Fax: The more expensive hotels will often be able to send and receive faxes on your behalf.

Internet cafés: Cafés and hotels increasingly have Wi-Fi hotspots, which allow anyone with their own laptop to log onto the Internet. ADSL connections are also becoming more common in hotels and again these are useful for those with their own computers. Many hotels have Internet-ready PCs for guests to use. There are public Internet terminals at the the Central Post Office (see Post) and the Estonian National Library (✉ Tõnismägi 2). The local tourist office will be able to point you in the direction of other Internet cafés/clubs.

Electricity

The power system is 220 volts, 50 AC. European two-pin round-pronged plugs are used.

Weights and Measures

Estonia uses the metric system.

Health Precautions

An excess of sun and alcohol are the worst problems encountered by most people visiting Estonia. In summer protect against the sun with

sunscreen, sunglasses and a hat; you should also drink plenty of water to avoid dehydration. Tap water is safe to drink. Precautions should also be taken against sexually transmitted diseases.

Personal Safety

Tallinn experiences its fair share of crime; fortunately most of this is petty crime like pickpocketing and bag snatching. Simple measures such as carrying your valuables securely and out of sight (the same applies to vehicles) should help keep you safe. If you are drunk you are more likely to become a victim of crime, so consume alcohol in moderation. Avoid walking alone in the dark and secluded spaces. If a crime is committed against you report it to the police immediately, particularly if you plan on claiming from your insurance company.

Emergencies

Fire: ☎ 112
Police: ☎ 112
Ambulance: ☎ 110

Etiquette

Attempting a few words in the local language and remembering your manners will always stand you in good stead.

Language

The national language is Estonian. Estonian is a Finno-Ugric language that has more in common with Finnish than with the languages of its Baltic State neighbours. It is a tricky language to learn, with 14 noun cases, but locals will appreciate your efforts, even simple pleasantries. Many of Tallinn's residents can speak English, particularly those employed in hotels, restaurants and cafés. Lots of younger Estonians are also fluent in English. Finnish and Russian are also widely spoken in Estonia.

INDEX OF SIGHTS

GENERAL INDEX

GENERAL INDEX

GENERAL INDEX

GENERAL INDEX